An Event-Based Science Module

OIL SPILL!

Student Edition

Russell G. Wright

PEARSON

Prentice Hall

Boston, Massachusetts
Upper Saddle River, New Jersey

The developers of Event-Based Science have been encouraged and supported at every step in the creative process by the superintendent and board of education of Montgomery County Public Schools, Rockville, Maryland (MCPS). The superintendent and board are committed to the systemic improvement of science instruction, grades preK–12. EBS is one of many projects undertaken to ensure the scientific literacy of all students.

The developers of *Oil Spill!* pay special tribute to the editors, publisher, and reporters of *USA TODAY*. Without their cooperation and support, the creation of this module would not have been possible.

The maps and tide charts in this volume are based on material from the National Oceanic and Atmospheric Administration.

"The Great Oil Spill Cleanup Contest" was adapted with permission from an activity developed by Elaine Hampton.

Photographs: Cover Michelle Barnes, Gamma Liaison; pages 3, 10, 11, 17, 33 AP/Wide World Photos; 34 *USA TODAY*; 2 Dorothy Hall; 5 Susan Eskite Maps; page 68 Frank Loose; pages 65, 66, 67, 69, 70, Mapping Specialists

This material is based upon work supported by the National Science Foundation under grant number MDR-9154094. Any opinions, findings, conclusions, or recommendations expressed in this publication are those of the Event-Based Science Project and do not necessarily reflect the views of the National Science Foundation.

Copyright © 2005 by the Event-Based Science Institute. Published by Pearson Education, Inc., publishing as Pearson Prentice Hall, Boston, Massachusetts 02116. All rights reserved. Printed in the United States of America. This publication is protected by copyright, and permission should be obtained from the publisher prior to any prohibited reproduction, storage in a retrieval system, or transmission in any form or by any means, mechanical, photocopying, recording, or likewise. The publisher hereby grants permission to reproduce pages 53 and 54 for classroom use only, the number not to exceed the number of students in each class. For information regarding permission(s), write to Event-Based Science Institute, Inc., 6609 Paxton Road, Rockville, MD 20850.

Pearson Prentice Hall™ is a trademark of Pearson Education, Inc.
Pearson® is a registered trademark of Pearson plc.
Prentice Hall® is a registered trademark of Pearson Education, Inc.

ISBN: 0-13-166648-7

3 4 5 6 7 8 9 10   10 09 08 07

Contents

Project Team	iv
Preface	v

The Story
Part 1	1
Part 2	8
Part 3	18
Part 4	31

The Task	4

Science Activities
Ocean Currents	14
"When Do We Sail, Captain?"	22
Who Lives Where?	29
How Much Can a Ship Carry?	38
Hands-on Harbor Profile	39

Discovery Files
Currents—Going with the Flow	13
Coriolis Force	16
Waves	20
The Tide Rises, the Tide Falls	25
The Boston Tea Party	25
Ocean Life Zones	27
Density and Buoyancy	35
"Squat" and Bernoulli's Principle	37
Making Charts Where No One Has Walked or Looked	42

On the Job
Economist	15
Harbormaster	21
Marine Biologist	26
Oceanographer	30
Readiness Planner	36
Tanker Captain	41

Optional Activities
Don't Eat That Fish!	43
The Great Oil Spill Cleanup Contest	44

Interdisciplinary Activities
Math: Estimating the Area of the Harbor	45
Math: Capacity of Oil Tankers	45
Social Studies: Is It Worth the Risk?	46
Technology Education: Oil Spill Research and Development	47

Performance Assessment
Writing to Persuade	48

Appendixes
Appendix A —Products Made from Oil	51
Appendix B —Oil Spill Contingency Plan	52
Appendix C —Tide Charts	59
Appendix D —Nautical Charts	65

Bibliography	71
Science Safety Rules	73

Project Team

Author
Russell G. Wright, with contributions from Barbara Sprungman, Leonard David, Deborah Fort, and the following teachers:

Richard Chirumbole, West Middle School, Westminster, Maryland
*Vivian H. Clyburn, Herbert Hoover Middle School, Potomac, Maryland
*Nell Jeter, Earle B. Wood Middle School, Rockville, Maryland
*Cynthia Johnson-Cash, Ridgeview Middle School, Gaithersburg, Maryland
*Jeanne S. Klugel, Col. E. Brooke Lee Middle School, Silver Spring, Maryland
*William R. Krayer, Gaithersburg High School, Gaithersburg, Maryland
*Marilyn Matthews, Gaithersburg Middle School, Gaithersburg, Maryland
*Carl Merry, Quince Orchard High School, North Potomac, Maryland
*Eugene M. Molesky, Ridgeview Middle School, Gaithersburg, Maryland
*John Senuta, Ridgeview Middle School, Gaithersburg, Maryland
*Sheila Shillinger, Montgomery Village Middle School, Gaithersburg, Maryland
*J. Martin Smiley, Gaithersburg Middle School, Gaithersburg, Maryland
*Clare E. Von Secker, Westland Middle School, Bethesda, Maryland
*Frank S. Weisel, Poolesville Junior/Senior High School, Poolesville, Maryland

Event/Site Support
Gary Holsten, Palmer, Alaska

Scientific Reviewer
Celso S. Barrientos, N.O.A.A.

Student Consultants
*Redland Middle School, Rockville, Maryland: Julia Ahn, Amanda Armah, Jerard Barnett, Mark Batipps, Giancarlo Begazo, Twana Brooks, Dean Chilton, Jonathan Codell, Daniel Elbaz, Tim Lewis, Erin McMullen, Kym Thompson
*Ridgeview Middle School, Gaithersburg, Maryland: Sean Shillinger, Jeffrey Hsii

Field-Test Teachers
Judith Basile and Karen Shugrue, Agawam Junior High School, Feeding Hills, Massachusetts
David Needham and Gloria Yost, Albert Einstein Middle School, Sacramento, California
Merah Burke, Edmonston-Westside High School, Baltimore, Maryland
Joanne Cannon and Adrianne Criminger, Lanier Middle School, Buford, Georgia
Cheryl Glotfelty and Von Mosser, Northern Middle School, Accident, Maryland
Rodney Clem and Elizabeth McDermott, Southern High School, Baltimore, Maryland
Mark Carlson and Amy Ressler, Westlane Middle School, Indianapolis, Indiana

EBS Advisory Committee
Dr. Eddie Anderson, National Aeronautic and Space Administration
Dr. Lynn Dierking, National Museum of American History
Mr. Bob Dubill, *USA TODAY*
Mr. Herbert Freiberger, United States Geological Survey
Ms. Joyce Gross, National Oceanic and Atmospheric Administration
Dr. Harry Herzer, National Aeronautic and Space Administration
Mr. Frank Ireton, American Geophysical Union
*Mr. Bill Krayer, Gaithersburg High School
Dr. Rocky Lopes, American Red Cross
*Dr. Jerry Lynch, John T. Baker Middle School
Ms. Virginia Major, United States Geological Survey
Ms. Marylyn P. McCabe, Federal Emergency Management Agency
Mr. John Ortman, United States Department of Energy
Dr. Noel Raufaste Jr., National Institute of Standards and Technology
Dr. Bill Sacco, Trianalytics Corporation
Mr. Ron Slotkin, United States Environmental Protection Agency

*Montgomery County Public Schools, Rockville, MD

Oil Spill!

Preface

The Event-Based Science Model

Oil Spill! is an oceanography unit that follows the Event-Based Science (EBS) Instructional Model. You will watch "live" television news coverage of the Exxon *Valdez* oil spill and read *USA TODAY* reports about it. Your discussions about the oil spill will show you and your teacher that you already know a lot about the Earth-science concepts involved in the event. Next, a real-world task puts you and your classmates in the roles of people who must use scientific knowledge and processes to solve a problem related to oil spills. You will probably need more information before you start the task. If you do, *Oil Spill!* provides hands-on activities and a variety of reading materials to give you some of the background you need. About halfway through the unit, you will be ready to begin the task. Your teacher will assign you a role to play and turn you and your team loose to complete the task. You will spend the rest of the time in this unit working on that task.

Scientific Literacy

Today, a literate citizen is expected to know more than how to read, write, and do simple arithmetic. Today, literacy includes knowing how to analyze problems, ask critical questions, and explain events. A literate citizen must also be able to apply scientific knowledge and processes to new situations. Event-Based Science allows you to practice these skills by placing the study of science in a meaningful context.

Knowledge cannot be transferred to your mind from the mind of your teacher, or from the pages of a textbook. Nor can knowledge occur in isolation from the other things you know about and have experienced in the real world. The Event-Based Science model is based on the idea that the best way to learn something is to be actively engaged in it.

Therefore, the Event-Based Science model simulates real-life events and experiences to make your learning more authentic and memorable. First, the event is brought to life through television news coverage. Viewing the news allows you to be there "as it happens," and that is as close as you can get to actually experiencing the event. Second, by simulating the kinds of teamwork and problem solving that occur every day in our work places and communities, you will experience the role that scientific knowledge and teamwork play in the lives of ordinary people. Thus *Oil Spill!* is built around simulations of real-life events and experiences that affected people's lives and environments dramatically.

In an Event-Based Science classroom, you become the workers, your product is a solution to a real problem, and your teacher is your coach, guide, and advisor. You will be assessed on how you use scientific processes and concepts to solve problems as well as on the quality of your work.

One of the primary goals of the EBS Project is to place the learning of science in a real-world context and to make the learning of science fun. You should not allow yourself to become frustrated. If you cannot find a specific piece of information, it's okay to be creative. For example, if you are working as the economist for your team and you cannot find the kinds of industries that are located in the community you're investigating, use your imagination, but keep it realistic. Base your response on the real places and things you know about. Just remember to identify your creations as fictional.

Student Resources

Oil Spill! is unlike a regular textbook. An Event-Based Science module tells a story about a real event; it has real newspaper articles about the event, and inserts that explain the scientific concepts involved in the event. It also contains laboratory investigations for you to conduct in your science class, and activities that you may do in English, math, social studies, or technology education classes. In addition, an Event-Based Science module gives you and your classmates a real-world task to do. The task is always done by teams of students, with each team member performing a real-life role while completing an important part of the task. The task cannot be completed without you and everyone else on your team doing their parts. The team approach allows you to share your knowledge and strengths. It also helps you learn to work with a team in a real-world situation. Today, most professionals work in teams.

Interviews with people who actually serve in the roles you are playing are scattered throughout the Event-Based Science module. Middle school students who actually experienced the event tell their stories throughout the module too.

Since this module is unlike a regular textbook, you have much more flexibility in using it.

- You may read **The Story** for enjoyment or to find clues that will help you tackle your part of the task.

- You may read selections from the **Discovery File** when you need help understanding something in the story or when you need help with the task.

- You may read all the **On the Job** features because you are curious about what professionals do, or you may read only the interview with the professional who works in the role you've chosen because it may give you ideas that will help you complete the task.

- You may read the **In the News** features because they catch your eye, or as part of your search for information.

- You will probably read all the **Student Voices** features because they are interesting stories told by middle school students like yourself.

Oil Spill! is also unlike regular textbooks in that the collection of resources found in it is not meant to be complete. You must find additional information from other sources, too. Textbooks, encyclopedias, pamphlets, magazine and newspaper articles, videos, films, filmstrips, computer databases, and people in your community are all potential sources of useful information. If you have access to the World Wide Web, you will want to visit the Event-Based Science home page (www.PHSchool.com/EBS), where you will find links to other sites around the world with information and people that will be very helpful to you. It is vital to your preparation as a scientifically literate citizen of the twenty-first century that you get used to finding information on your own.

The shape of a new form of science education is beginning to emerge, and the Event-Based Science Project is leading the way. We hope you enjoy your experience with this module as much as we enjoyed developing it.

—Russell G. Wright, Ed.D.
Project Director and Principal Author

THE STORY—PART 1

Exxon *Valdez*: The Big Spill!

Riding low in the water, its inner tanks held millions of gallons of crude oil. Water slapped against the ship's hull as the giant supertanker pushed through the cold midnight air at a steady speed of 12 knots. Attempting to avoid ice in the outbound shipping lane, the tanker's captain plotted a new course—a route that would sail the tanker straight into the history books.

A crewman first spotted the red light that flashed every few seconds in the darkness off the bow on the ship's right side. Indeed, if the ship had been in safe waters, the flashing red beacon would have been to its left. It was a warning signal that meant bad news that early morning.

Stretching over three football fields in length, the huge ship could not be navigated clear of trouble in time. Nearly two miles are needed to bring such a supertanker to a stop. The ship shuddered. A muffled sound of grinding metal and a popping noise pierced the stillness of the night and rippled through the innards of the supertanker.

Five stories below the water's surface (about 50 feet) the keel of the ship impaled itself on a rocky underwater reef. The ship's liquid cargo of more than 62 million gallons of crude oil started gushing into the cold sea at a rate of about 20,000 gallons per hour! The tanker was in trouble and a disaster was in the making.

So began the largest and most devastating oil spill in U.S. history.

The catastrophic accident that happened at 12:04 A.M. on March 24, 1989, in Prince William Sound on the southern coast of Alaska will long be remembered, not only for the environ-mental havoc it caused, but for the many lessons learned that have altered how nations deal with oil spillage.

When the single-hulled, 987-foot-long Exxon *Valdez* (pronounced "val-deez") ran aground on Bligh Reef, about 25 miles from the port of Valdez, Alaska, five large gashes in the ship breached eight of the eleven cargo holds on the vessel. The two largest holes were 8 feet by 15 feet and 20 feet by 6 feet. Before the hemorrhaging of oil could be controlled, just under 11 million gallons of unprocessed oil poured into the water. It took nearly fifteen hours before initial cleanup crews reached the area. Available equipment brought to the disaster site was quickly overpowered by the magnitude of the spill. Wind-whipped waters rapidly spread the sticky crude outward from the grounded Exxon *Valdez*, making it difficult to corral the floating oil.

The impact of the spill was devastating. Thick patches of crude oil covered miles of water. Some 1,500 miles of shoreline were fouled with gooey oil. The oil traveled as far as 600 miles from the Exxon *Valdez* grounding.

One after another, coastal regions fell victim to the ecologically damaging oil spill. Hardest hit by the oil spill were the coastlines of Prince William Sound, the Kenai Peninsula, lower Cook Inlet, the Kodiak Archipelago, and the Alaska Peninsula. In total, part of one national forest, four national wildlife refuges, three national parks, five state parks, four state critical habitat areas, and one

➤ continued on page 2

STUDENT VOICES

I remember standing on the top of the beach looking down; it looked like someone had laid a thin black sheet of plastic in all directions. It made me realize the dangers of living in a technological world.

EM KRUEGER
CHENEGA BAY & ICY BAY
PALMER, ALASKA

▶ continued from page 1

state game sanctuary felt the slimy fingerprints of oil seeping from the torn hull of the Exxon *Valdez*.

The true victim of the spill was the Alaskan wildlife. As many as 645,000 birds, 6,000 marine mammals, and millions of salmon and herring were killed. In addition, some 40,000 Alaskan natives, particularly local fishermen, had their way of life affected by the tanker's mishap.

This environmental disaster sparked a massive cleanup response costing over $2 billion, a lawsuit that led to $900 million being placed in a natural resources settlement fund, and the Oil Pollution Act of 1990.

Tragically, the saga of the Exxon *Valdez,* like oil mixed with water, was a bad blend of confusion layered atop bureaucracy, poor judgment, and even a touch of alcohol. ■

Discussion Questions

- What is crude oil and where does it come from?
- What useful products come from crude oil?
- When crude oil spills, does it float or sink?
- Tides and currents affect the spread of spilled oil. What are tides and what are currents?
- Why do you think oil spills kill marine life?
- Is it possible to clean up an oil spill completely?

IN THE NEWS

Oil prices rise as spill area widens

By Calvin Lawrence Jr.
and Judy Keen
USA TODAY

Crude oil prices hit their highest levels in 19 months Monday, as cleanup of the USA's worst oil spill stalled in bad weather off Alaska.

Winds spread oil over 125 square miles from where the supertanker Exxon Valdez ran aground Friday. The gunk has shut down the nearby port of Valdez, terminus for the Alaskan pipeline.

Alaska accounts for 25 percent of U.S. domestic oil production.

▶ Most affected by the price increases will be consumers on the West Coast, where much of the Alaska oil is used.

Even if the port reopens today, West Coast drivers can expect gasoline prices at the pump to rise 1 or 2 cents within the week, says Sal Gilbertie of oil trader Elders Futures Inc.

▶ The rest of us can breathe easier. Analysts say Monday's jump in crude oil prices was an overreaction by the market.

"It's a temporary aberration," says analyst Joseph Ancona at Daniels & Bell Inc. in St. Louis.

In oil futures trading Monday, the price of West Texas Intermediate crude, the USA's benchmark grade, went up 38 cents to $20.53 a barrel.

Also on Monday:

▶ Alaska Gov. Steve Cowper said there may be a new crisis if the port doesn't reopen by week's end because oil storage tanks at the port of Valdez will be full.

"I think that things would get critical in three to four days," he said. Pipeline flow has been slowed to 800,000 barrels a day. Normal: 1.6 million.

▶ Oil already washed ashore on several islands.

▶ "Exxon owes an explanation," said Interior Secretary Manuel Lujan Jr. "They will be responsible for a cleanup. There's no excuse at all for someone who was not qualified to be at the helm of that ship."

Exxon had said their ship was piloted by a third mate without proper certification when it struck a reef.

USA TODAY, 28 MARCH 1989

2   *Oil Spill!*

IN THE NEWS

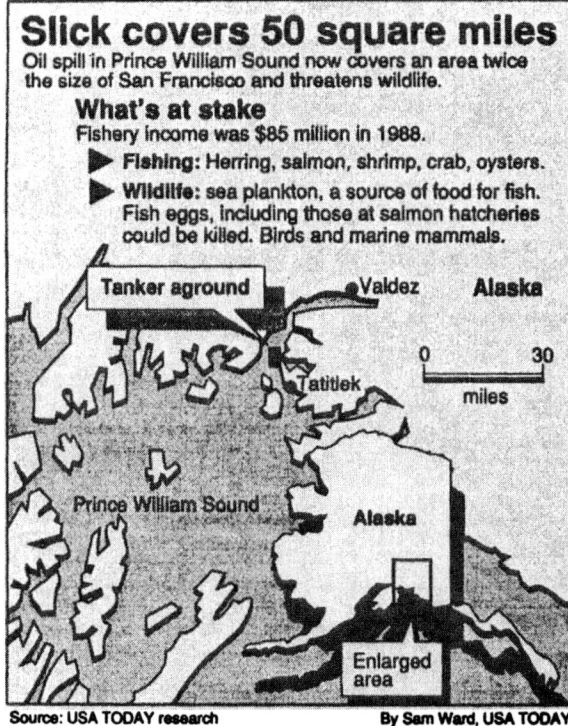

Slick covers 50 square miles
Oil spill in Prince William Sound now covers an area twice the size of San Francisco and threatens wildlife.

What's at stake
Fishery income was $85 million in 1988.
▶ **Fishing:** Herring, salmon, shrimp, crab, oysters.
▶ **Wildlife:** sea plankton, a source of food for fish. Fish eggs, including those at salmon hatcheries could be killed. Birds and marine mammals.

Source: USA TODAY research — By Sam Ward, USA TODAY

Alaska oil spill: Fears come true

By Judy Keen and Mike McQueen
USA TODAY

Alaskans who live near the site of the USA's worst oil spill fear their remote hideaway never will recover.

"It's a real tragedy — our worst fears come true," says Valdez fisherman Dick Feenstra of Friday's spill.

"This is a disaster of great enormity," says environmentalist and charter boat operator Nancy Lethcoe of Valdez.

Angered by what they believe was tardy response and dissatisfied because there's little they can do to stem its deadly effects, Valdez's 3,600 residents spent the holiday weekend worrying.

"There is this frustration that not a whole lot is being done in terms of containment and cleanup," says city manager Doug Griffin.

Valdez has suffered an Easter disaster before — 25 years ago, 31 died in a Good Friday earthquake.

Valdez — a wealthy boom town since completion of the Alaska pipeline in 1977 — depends on oil. Three-fourths of those in town work for the Alyeska Pipeline Service Co.

Hundreds more fish or work in fish processing plants. Sunday, fishermen met with Exxon officials about compensation for lost catch.

Fishermen say the herring, salmon, shrimp and crab they depend on will be the spill's first victims. But the toll could mount through 1991, when pink salmon spawned this year should return to the sound:
▶ "It could cost us our livelihoods," says Feenstra.
▶ "It'll take years to build the fish stocks back up," says Ray Cesarini, owner of a fish processing firm.
▶ "The mood is total disbelief, anger and frustration,"

GROUNDED TANKER: A smaller ship unloads oil from the Exxon Valdez, which ran aground Friday in Prince William Sound.

says Peggy Day, a 26-year resident who worries the mess will be forgotten when the oil dissipates. "I just hope that, later, they don't think because the water looks pretty that all is fine and dandy."

Oil pollution could reduce the harvest and bad publicity about the spill could lead to lower sales, fishermen fear.

"This could ruin our reputation in Asian markets for years to come," says Jim Brown, a local netter.

Oil industry publisher Karen Coburn says tourism and the oil industry could be hurt: "The point of going to Alaska is to look at the pristine wilderness — not an oil spill."

Coburn, publisher of the *Oil Spill Intelligence Report* newsletter, also says the spill could turn public opinion against the oil industry.

Oil production is at 800,000 barrels daily — 1.2 million barrels below normal — because officials had to close a storage terminal at Valdez.

Eighty-two percent of the state's $2.3 billion budget comes from oil taxes.

Calculating the USA's worst oil spills

The Exxon Valdez tanker accident spilled between 10 million and 11 million gallons of oil. The worst oil spills in U.S. history, according to records kept since 1976:

1. Nov. 1, 1979, Burmah Agate tanker, Galveston Bay, Texas, 10.7 million gallons of oil burned or spilled when two ships collided.

2. Dec. 15, 1976, Argo Merchant tanker, Massachusetts' southeast coast, 7.6 million gallons spilled when ship ran aground.

3. Nov. 6, 1985, exploratory well, Ranger, Texas, 6.3 million gallons of oil spilled after a blow-out.

4. Jan. 2, 1988, Ashland Oil Co., above-ground storage tank, Jefferson Borough, Pa., 3.8 million gallons spilled when tank ruptured.

5. July 30, 1984, Alvenus tanker, Cameron, La., 2.8 million gallons spilled after ship ran aground.

Source: Golob's Oil Pollution Bulletin

The Story—Part 1

The Task

Consulting for the Oil Industry

Few of us have escaped the experience of being responsible for a serious "milk spill" at the dinner table. Fortunately, damage is usually minimal and the cleanup procedure is a quick and easy process. No long-lasting, serious consequences plague you. Oil spills, on the other hand, are a much more serious matter.

For the next five weeks, you and your classmates are the highly respected analysts of Port Consultants, Inc. Your company has earned national recognition for your expertise in investigating and selecting sites for future oil terminals.

You and your colleagues followed the Exxon *Valdez* oil spill events from the start and were asked to testify at one of the U.S. Congressional hearings on the *Valdez* oil spill. You have proved your competence both nationally and among your peers.

So here are the details of the task before you. Your class has been divided into six teams. Each team will conduct an in-depth study and analysis of one of the following six ports as a potential site for an oil terminal:

West coast:	San Francisco, California
	San Diego, California
Southern coast:	Galveston, Texas
	Pensacola, Florida
East coast:	Charleston, South Carolina
	Baltimore, Maryland

Your team must prepare a fifteen-minute presentation that will include a summary of your findings including all parts outlined in the letter from Crude Oil Petroleum Company (on page 6).

After all presentations have been made, you will review the pros and cons of each site and recommend one city on each of the nation's three coasts that you judge to be the best choice for a future oil terminal.

Teams will include the following experts:

Harbormaster
Physical oceanographer
Marine biologist
Economist
Risk planner

Choosing Your Expert Role

You and your site investigation team members will each submit a prioritized list to your teacher with your role preferences (first choice, and so on). First choices will be assigned if possible.

Before you decide on your preferred role, read over the Expert Task descriptions and make sure you are willing and able to meet the responsibilities of the role. Not only will your teammates be counting on you, but so will whole populations of the cities you are evaluating.

Expert Tasks

Harbormaster: Prepare a presentation that describes the harbor of your city in terms of
   1. topography of the harbor bottom
   2. recommended location of the oil unloading facility
   3. type(s) of ships the harbor can accommodate.

Physical oceanographer: Prepare a presentation that describes
   1. local currents
   2. wave action in the harbor
   3. seasonal weather changes
   4. tidal influences on the harbor.

Marine biologist: Prepare a presentation on the effects of an oil spill on life in the harbor with emphasis on the commercial fishing industry.

Economist: Prepare a presentation on
   1. history of the area
   2. the impact of a new oil terminal on business
   3. future growth of the region.

Risk planner: Prepare a contingency (backup) plan that includes:
1. human, material, and financial factors involved in a cleanup
2. reaction time, worst-case scenario, priority procedures
3. networks of communication
4. suggested port-operation guidelines.

While teams work together to prepare the most useful and fair assessments of the competing cities, experts from the six teams will also meet as subgroups to compare notes and findings. Your teacher may also choose to assign some whole-class activities. At the end of approximately four weeks, each team will present an oral assessment of its city's potential as an oil terminal. These reports should include charts, maps, interviews, graphs, models, videotapes, and so on. You will have only fifteen minutes for your presentation.

The Exxon *Valdez* oil spill is a case study of what can go wrong. The videotapes and *USA Today* articles may provide clues that will help you with your task. Refer to the preface on how best to use this module as a resource.

Your school and city library, science textbooks available for reference, your teacher's files, and other materials will also be essential research tools as you work to prepare your team report. Besides the scientific principles underlying such phenomena as tides, marine life, and ocean floor topography, you will need to consider such matters as economics, industrial trends, and lines of communication.

Although you will eventually be deciding on one city for each of the three coasts, you are not in competition with other teams or other cities since you and your classmates work for the same consulting firm. You are making the best possible case, showing both the pros and cons, and not attempting to influence the choice of your city over another.

This is an important decision. Keep in mind the Exxon *Valdez* spill. Was the city as well prepared as it should have been in terms of the accident itself and the cleanup procedure? As scientists and economists, your concern for the financial benefits a terminal would bring must be weighed against many other factors.

The Charge

The two letters on the following pages provide a detailed description of what is required of your team when conducting the in-depth study of your city.

The decision you make will bring jobs and prosperity to the cities selected at a time when the state of the economy is a challenge for everyone. The importance of doing your best, and considering all the possibilities, will become evident as you see how your decisions can influence the quality of life for millions of people, as well as the plants and animals, in the cities that you and your colleagues recommend.

As you work on this task, you will find that there are many important considerations when confronted with a disaster. There is a possibility that sometime in the future you will be faced with a disaster, and that your informed decisions could save lives.

COPCo

**Crude Oil Petroleum Company
Houston, Texas 77598
Phone 1-800 OILWELL**

**Margaret Johnson
President**

Mr. Julio Gonzales
Port Consultants, Inc.
22 Expert Street
Proficiency, Delaware 19963

Dear Mr. Gonzales:

COPCo is considering building oil loading and unloading facilities on each coast of the United States. Our site selection committee has chosen six possible ports for the new terminals. They are:

San Francisco, California	Pensacola, Florida
San Diego, California	Charleston, South Carolina
Galveston, Texas	Baltimore, Maryland

Please direct your staff to conduct in-depth studies of each city, provide us with summaries of their findings, and recommend three (one per coast) as sites for our oil terminals. Be sure to include the following:

- Specific harbor characteristics of the area including topography, location of the loading/unloading facility, and the types of ships the harbor can accommodate.
- Physical-ocean characteristics of the area including local currents, wave action in the harbor and along the coast, seasonal weather changes, and tidal influences on the harbor.
- Biological factors of the area such as ocean life zones, life cycles of ocean plants and animals, coast profiles for each city, and the possible effects of an accidental oil spill on each.
- Economic factors of the area including the impact of a new oil terminal on business, future fuel needs in the area, and possible new industries.
- Emergency-preparedness measures needed, such as human, material, and monetary factors involved in a cleanup effort, as well as contingency plans, reaction time, priority procedures, communication networks, and suggested port operation guidelines.

With this information, we hope to safely expand our operations into new areas and increase our profits.

Enclosed is a check for you to begin the study. The balance will be paid upon delivery.

Sincerely,

M. Johnson
Margaret Johnson

Port Consultants, Inc.
22 Expert Street
Proficiency, Delaware 19963

MEMORANDUM

To: San Francisco Team   Pensacola Team
      San Diego Team   Charleston Team
      Galveston Team   Baltimore Team

From: Julio Gonzales, President and General Manager *JG*

Date: _____

Attached you will find a letter from Margaret Johnson, president of Crude Oil Petroleum Company (COPCo), requesting our services. I have personally selected you and the other members of your team because of the unique talents you bring to the task.

Review Ms. Johnson's letter with your team. If you need help before you start, develop a short list of questions you need to have answered before we begin. We will discuss questions and begin background investigation tomorrow. Teams must be ready to give a fifteen-minute summary report in four weeks.

I suggest that experts from each city team meet together periodically in designated conference areas:

     Harbormasters (team leaders)   Conference Area 1
     Physical Oceanographers   Conference Area 2
     Marine Biologists   Conference Area 3
     Economists   Conference Area 4
     Risk Planners   Conference Area 5

Your team must be prepared to address all items requested by Ms. Johnson.

The company library will be made available for teams to use as needed.

Please have your analyses ready to present four weeks from today. Be prepared to support your presentation with charts and graphs. Each expert on your team will have three minutes, the team will have fifteen minutes. There will be five additional minutes for questions.

The Story—Part 2
Managing a Mess

The immense oil and gas reservoir near Prudhoe Bay on the Arctic Coast was discovered in 1968. Geologists estimated that upwards of 10 billion barrels of oil (1 barrel of oil equals 42 gallons) could be recovered from the locale—a bounty of oil twice as large as any other deposit in North America!

But to safely move that "black gold" or "Texas tea"—as television's Beverly Hillbillies called it—across Alaska's frozen North Slope required the construction of the huge Trans-Alaska pipeline, costing $7.7 billion to build. An ice-free port at a northern site closest to Prudhoe Bay was selected as the oil-receiving end of the pipeline. The first oil began flowing out of Prudhoe Bay into the port of Valdez in June of 1977 through 800 miles of pipeline pushed by sets of pumping stations along the way. The payoff? The State of Alaska receives more than 80 percent of its yearly revenue from companies that rent state-owned land to extract the oil. One-quarter of all U.S. domestic oil is produced in Alaska.

When the oil-filled Exxon *Valdez* pulled away from its loading terminal in Valdez on March 23, 1989, headed for an Exxon refinery in Long Beach, California, the tanker was under the command of Joseph Hazelwood. Hazelwood and several other crew members of the Exxon *Valdez* were fatigued after working long hours that enabled them to chalk up lucrative amounts of overtime.

Shortly after the Exxon *Valdez* edged out of the Alyeska Pipeline Service Company terminal in Valdez, Captain Hazelwood, an experienced mariner who had navigated Exxon ships for over twenty years, turned over his duties to others just a half-hour before the accident. By excusing himself to his cabin below, and leaving an uncertified crewman to help pilot the huge vessel, Hazelwood violated specific Exxon rules. Furthermore, it was later determined that Hazelwood's blood-alcohol level indicated that he was intoxicated while in charge of the ship. A half-empty bottle of whisky was found in his quarters at the time of the oil spill.

After missing a critical turn, the Exxon *Valdez* struck the navigational hazard known as Bligh Reef. First attempts to free the tanker from its devastating underwater perch failed. Oil began to bubble up to the surface from underneath through rips in the ship's metal skin.

Response to the Exxon *Valdez* crisis was slow in coming. Contingency plans written 12 years earlier were put into action. Those procedures called for Alyeska (a consortium of seven major oil companies that owns the terminal at Valdez as well as the Alaskan pipeline itself) to respond to any spills. But 14 hours would pass before Alyeska's cleanup squad could begin operations. By then winds, waves, and currents had spread the oil over 6 square miles—equal to nearly 4,000 acres!

An armada of equipment eventually reached the Exxon *Valdez*. Many miles of sausage-like oil containment barriers, known as booms, were hastily deployed in the water. These were designed to encircle the oil as it floated on the water's surface by

STUDENT VOICES

I remember a feeling of complete futility. I desperately wanted to do something, but was too limited in ability and position. Prevention of spills must be the prime focus. A comprehensive cleanup plan, however, must be set up.

JEFFREY KRUEGER
CHENEGA BAY & ICY BAY
PALMER, ALASKA

either containing or absorbing the spillage. Numbers of skimmers attempted to siphon off or absorb quantities of the released oil, recapturing the substance for storage on oil-recovery boats. Other equipment was put into action, such as dredges to suck up floating oil and remove tainted seabed sediment. But the daunting magnitude of the *Valdez* oil spill soon overpowered the emergency teams and the ability of the equipment to gulp up the floating oil.

In a matter of hours, thanks to a blend of choppy waters, gusty winds, and ocean currents, the oil spill began its devastating crawl toward landfall. The currents, moving like slow but powerful rivers through the oil-laden water, took over as captain of the Exxon *Valdez*'s liberated cargo, piloting the massive spill toward the shores.

Agitated by the wind, the spilled oil was whipped into a thick, goo-like substance, with the consistency

➤ continued on page 10

IN THE NEWS

Gas prices have been slow to follow

But by June, expect price increases nationwide

By David Craig and David Landis
USA TODAY

It's one of the economy's best kept secrets.

The price of crude oil has risen more than 50% since late November. Yet, we've barely noticed.

Even though the USA consumes one-third of all oil produced in the non-communist world — more than 18 million barrels a day — the impact of the recent rise in crude prices has been minimal so far. That's remarkable if you remember what happened in the 1970s. When crude prices soared following the 1973 Arab oil embargo and the 1979 Iranian revolution, the economy went into a tailspin, and panicky drivers spent hours in line at gas stations, waiting to top off their tanks.

"After the last oil crisis, there were a lot of changes made to reduce our dependence on oil," says economist Kim Rupert of MMS International Inc. "At the moment, there's enough leeway in the economy so that (the crude increases) are being absorbed."

West Texas intermediate, the USA's benchmark grade of crude, closed at $19.99 a barrel Wednesday in futures trading on the New York Mercantile Exchange. A few days before Thanksgiving, it traded as low as $12.98 a 42-gallon barrel. Consumers aren't screaming because gasoline prices haven't kept up with oil prices. Gas prices averaged $1 a gallon in March, the same price as November. One big reason we haven't seen higher gas prices: They already are relatively high. Although crude oil prices started a slide in summer 1988 that lasted until Thanksgiving, refiners didn't cut gas prices because they didn't have to. Demand was high, and supplies were tight. Last July, for instance, crude prices were 23% below levels a year earlier, but gasoline prices actually had risen 1% over that period, says Ed Rothschild of the Citizen/Labor Energy Coalition.

That's going to change soon. Some western parts of the USA are about to get socked with big increases in gas prices — as much as 20 cents a gallon in the next few weeks. Much of the gas price increase is due to a temporary factor — the disastrous Exxon oil spill in Alaska, which temporarily cut off supplies to some West Coast refineries. But other factors also are at work: We're using more gas, and refineries are straining to keep up with the demand.

In addition, there's little optimism that crude prices will fall back dramatically any time soon. For once, the usually quarrelsome members of the Organization of Petroleum Exporting Countries are keeping their oil production under control. OPEC signed a six-month production accord last fall that took effect Jan. 1. At the midpoint — this very week — it has held up remarkably well, much better than anyone had predicted. That should keep crude prices from tumbling. "There's definitely a realization that OPEC is getting along a lot better than it has in a long time," says analyst George Gaspar of Robert W. Baird & Co.

In addition, eight non-OPEC oil-producing nations, known collectively as NOPEC, have reduced their production by 200,000 barrels a day at OPEC's behest. Rising prices might prompt NOPEC members to increase production, but Gaspar says OPEC will pressure them to keep their production down.

If crude prices stay where they are, everything from airplane tickets to household plastic goods could become more expensive. Jet fuel, for example, already is 7 cents a gallon above its 1988 average. "Airlines might eat part of that increase, but they're also going to have to pass some along," says Lew Townsend, associate editor of *Aviation Daily*.

What's in store as summer rolls around? Here's a look:

▶ **Crude prices:** Analysts say crude should trade between $17 and $21 a barrel this summer.

Nervousness about the impact of the Alaskan oil spill helped crude prices pierce $20 a barrel last month for the first time since October 1987. An American Petroleum Institute report this week showed the fears were justified. The nation's oil inventories fell to 324.6 million barrels for the week ended March 31 — a 12.8 million-barrel drop from the week before — in the aftermath of the spill, the report said. But Wednesday, the Trans Alaska Pipeline resumed its normal production levels of 2 million barrels a day. That should ease supply worries.

But crude prices will remain strong because demand for oil is rising. The 13-nation cartel pumped an estimated 19.7 million barrels a day in March — above its self-imposed quota of 18.5 million barrels a day — yet prices kept rising.

"There's no overproduction in the world right now," Gaspar says. He predicts that OPEC will increase its production quota to 20 million barrels a day for the second half of the year to keep prices from rising above $21 a barrel.

OPEC doesn't want prices to rise too high. Higher prices make drilling for oil in the USA and elsewhere more profitable, and OPEC doesn't want the competition, says Adam Sieminski, analyst at Washington Analysis Corp.

Also, OPEC is very aware of the economic repercussions of high oil prices. "They don't want to be responsible for helping push the U.S. into a recession with higher oil prices," Sieminski says. "Ultimately it's as bad for them, if not worse" because recession leads to reduced demand for OPEC oil, he says.

▶ **Gas prices:** The bad news: They're going to continue rising through the summer.

Last week, oil buyers on the West Coast spot market, panicky about the cutoff of shipments from Alaska, were paying wholesale prices of more than $1 a gallon, nearly double prices from a week earlier. The result: increases of up to 23 cents a gallon by Memorial Day on the West Coast, 5 cents to 15 cents elsewhere, says Tom Kloza, editor of the *Oil Price Information Service* newsletter. "I don't think those prices will stick where they are, but I doubt they'll go back to where they were a week ago," Kloza says. But once concern over the Alaskan disaster dies down, other factors will remain to keep gas prices rising. Brisk consumer demand is just one of them.

USA TODAY, 6 APRIL 1989

▶ continued from page 9

of a "chocolate mousse." This floating goo is actually composed of air bubbles and water surrounded by oil. Not only did this floating material cause problems for cleanup equipment, but also many seabirds and sea otters were exposed to the "mousse," and there were numerous casualties among the wildlife. Much of the oily goo found its way to the Kenai and Kodiak areas.

Also, hydrodynamics was in action as only 10 percent of the spilled oil rose above the waterline, just like an iceberg with much of its mass hidden below the ocean surface. Moreover, the *Valdez* oil slick fragmented into numerous smaller patches, or formed into soft, tan-colored "tarballs," again making cleanup operations all the more complex. The Alaskan crude oil became difficult for pumps to handle as temperatures reached

IN THE NEWS

Liquor use probed in oil spill

Hearing scheduled next week

By Judy Keen
USA TODAY

Investigators focused Monday on reports of drinking aboard the tanker that dumped 10 million gallons of oil in Prince William Sound near Valdez, Alaska.

Exxon Shipping Co. president Frank Iarossi admitted Capt. Joseph Hazelwood of Huntington, N.Y., violated company policy by staying in his cabin while an unauthorized crewman, Third Mate Gregory Cousins of Tampa, Fla., piloted the ship through the bay and into a reef.

Iarossi wouldn't comment on reports Hazelwood was drinking alcohol, but said the captain had a prior problem.

The National Transportation Safety Board is investigating and some state officials have called for a criminal investigation. NTSB hearings will be held next week in Anchorage.

Drucella Anderson of the NTSB said tests of the crew may prove useless because they were taken up to 10 hours after the ship ran aground.

Also Monday:
▶ Iarossi said he could no longer promise oil wouldn't taint beaches or that the 42 million gallons of oil still aboard could be removed. "Frankly, we are a little overwhelmed."

The oil spill threatens 3,000 miles of coastline. A few oil-fouled birds have been spotted near an island where some oil has washed ashore.

▶ Exxon officials now believe the tanker had struck one rock and already was leaking when it struck a second rock and ran aground.

Alaskans' frustration is mounting. Among the critics is Gov. Steve Cowper.

"Exxon caused this spill and

PUMPING: Tankers remove oil from the Exxon Valdez Monday. Winds up to 70 mph shifted the leaking ship 12 degrees.
By Rob Stapleton, AP

LIVELIHOOD THREATENED: Fred Tiedeman, who lives in the village of Tatitlek, worries he no longer will be able to make a living fishing the sound where 10 million gallons of oil were spilled.
By Rob Stapleton, AP

Alyeska Pipeline Co.'s slow response made it worse than it had to be," he said.

"If the spill had been contained quickly after the tanker ran on the reef, it's probable we would not have it spread all over Prince William Sound."

Valdez Mayor John Devens says Exxon officials promised him they'd "pull out all the stops" before weather interfered Monday. The city can't touch a $16 million emergency fund — taxes on oil firms — because state officials challenged the tax's legality.

"What we want to do is get that · · · oil cleaned up off that water," says Devens.

The fishing industry says international buyers already are balking at buying fish from the sound. Oil fumes were sickening volunteers helping in their own boats.

80% of oil isn't recovered

By Mike McQueen
USA TODAY

Oil spills generally are mopped up quickly, but only about 20 percent of the spill is recovered, experts say.

"The oil's still there. The particles are too small to be seen," says National Wildlife Federation's Erik Olson.

Wind and waves break up the remaining 80 percent, with bacteria feeding on the lingering sludge.

Since a 6,000-barrel spill near Santa Barbara, Calif., shocked the nation in 1969, several spills have caused more serious problems:

▶ A 231,000-gallon spill last December off Washington's southwest coast killed 10,000 birds and fouled hundreds of miles of pristine beach north to Canada.

▶ Wind blew a 7.6 million gallon spill into the open Atlantic from Nantucket Island, Mass., in 1976. Bad weather prolonged cleanup nine days.

▶ Water supplies on the Ohio and Monongahela rivers were tainted as 1 million gallons of oil floated down river in an Ashland Oil tank collapse near Pittsburgh.

Some say hard-to-handle spills are a result of shipping oil by sea. "We should be moving oil by land because at least on land . . . we can contain it," says Steven Swartz of the Center for Marine Conservation.

Representatives of the environmental group Greenpeace moved Monday to protect beaches. "So far, very few beaches have been oiled. I don't know how long our luck will hold," says Hild Sandstede.

"It's gone beyond disgruntled to absolutely discouraged and hopeless," says charter boat owner Nancy Lethcoe.

"We cannot believe the snowball effect of the inadequate initial response."

USA TODAY, 31 MARCH 1989

10   Oil Spill!

about 0 to 5 degrees Celsius in the frigid waters. Problems in cleanup operations were further compounded as the total volume of the frothy oil/water emulsion reached several times the volume of the initial oil spill.

Realizing the seriousness of the situation, Alyeska turned to Exxon Shipping, a wholly owned subsidiary of the Exxon Corporation, for much needed help. Being the responsible shipowner of the Exxon *Valdez*, the Exxon firm took charge of cleanup operations. Eyeing this change of hands was the U.S. Coast Guard, itself responsible for directing tanker traffic, writing oil-spill plans, regulating tankers, licensing crews, as well as coordinating cleanup procedures and prodding those involved to respond faster. Also taking part in staging the oil-spill response were various federal, state, and commercial organizations.

However, as the oil spread hour by hour, day by day, so too did the finger pointing, accusations of wrongdoing, and total confusion. Critics charged inept handling of the situation by all parties, thereby slowing and complicating any hope of deploying an effective campaign of countermeasures.

Two days after the *Valdez* went aground, Exxon took over cleanup operations. Although the call for needed equipment was answered from around the world, mechanical cleanup of the oil spill was no match for the huge volume of oil to be recovered. Thousands of people were called into action as oil herders and scavengers.

In the end, most of the oil aboard Exxon *Valdez* was successfully off-loaded, a procedure called "lightering." In total, about one-fifth of the crude oil housed in the tanker had been released into the natural environment.

Toward the close of 1989, the combined recovery effort of government and industry accounted for just 32,500 gallons of oil being removed from the water—a literal drop in the oil bucket compared to the well over 10 million gallons of crude that spread over water and precious coastlines. ■

IN THE NEWS

Oil probe: 3rd mate at helm

By Andrea Stone
USA TODAY

The captain of the grounded tanker responsible for the largest oil spill in USA history had left the bridge, violating company policy, says an Exxon Shipping Co. spokesman.

The tanker Exxon Valdez, which ran aground about 12:30 a.m. local time Friday near the port of Valdez, has spewed 11 million gallons into wildlife-rich Prince William Sound.

Late Sunday, Alaska's governor declared it a disaster area.

Investigators are focusing on the tanker's crew, which has been tested for drug use.

At the time of the accident, the third mate was in control. "It's Exxon's policy that in the waters that the ship was located in, the captain should have been on the bridge," says Exxon Shipping's Brian Dunphy.

The off-course tanker had left a traffic lane to avoid ice.

Meanwhile, Alaska's environmental chief Sunday ordered Exxon to clean up the spill — or his state will.

"Too little, too late, too many excuses" was how Dennis Kelso summed up the response of Exxon and Alyeska Pipeline Service Co. to the spill.

Exxon says it will pay for cleanup and damage claims, which could run as high as $100 million, estimates show.

Among Alaska's concerns:
▶ Use of chemical dispersants to clean the 100-square-mile slick could poison fish.
▶ Although Exxon says the environmental impact so far is "minimal," 95 oiled birds and two otters have been spotted.
▶ The $85 million fishing industry, including salmon, herring and crab, also is in danger.

Port Valdez remains closed and no oil is leaving the sole terminus of the 800-mile Trans-Alaska pipeline. Alaska produces one-fourth of USA oil.

USA TODAY, 27 MARCH 1989

Huge bail for tanker skipper

By Dick Yarwood via AP
HAZELWOOD: At hearing

Judge calls spill 'global catastrophe'

By Mike McQueen
USA TODAY

Fired Exxon tanker Capt. Joseph Hazelwood was held Wednesday on $1 million bond or $500,000 cash on misdemeanor criminal charges in the nation's worst oil spill.

The cash bail was 20 times what prosecutors requested.

"We have a man-made destruction that has not been equaled, probably, since Hiroshima," said Suffolk County, N.Y., Judge Kenneth Rohl.

The judge said although the charges are only misdemeanors, "We are not talking about someone breaking someone's windshield. We are talking about a global catastrophe."

Hazelwood, 42, left Alaska last week before the state ordered him arrested on drinking and negligence charges in the tanker crash near Valdez.

Hazelwood has 30 days to prepare for a hearing on extradition to Alaska, where the charges carry fines of $10,000 and 27 months in jail.

USA TODAY, 6 APRIL 1989

OIL SPILL

A LOOK AT WHAT'S BEING DONE TO CLEAN UP THE SPILL

How oil is cleaned up, what's done for animals

Only 1 percent of the 10 million gallons that spilled into Alaska's once-pristine Prince William Sound has been recovered, state environmental officials say.

The spill is so unwieldy, they say, that crews are working primarily to save only vital salmon hatcheries near Valdez, Alaska. The three large hatcheries are preparing to release 35 million baby salmon.

Why was so little oil recovered?

Exxon says bad weather — high winds and rough seas — hampered cleanup efforts. Fishermen and state environmental officials say Exxon didn't make quick decisions about how to clean up the spill and that there wasn't enough cleanup equipment nearby.

What equipment is being used to clean up the remaining oil?

Private fishermen and others are using booms — inflatable synthetic devices that capture the oil — to keep the sludge from spreading to the hatcheries. Booms are among the most commonly used oil cleanup devices.

What else is used with booms?

The booms trap the oil and then small boats — called skimmers — maneuver near the edge of the booms and pump both water and oil into special machines aboard the boat. Those machines separate the oil from the water.

What happens when waves carry the oil ashore?

Crews used shovels and rakes to scoop up oil-tainted sand and absorbent cotton pads to soak up oil.

What effect does the oil have on salmon?

The salmon harvest starts in June, but fishermen say it's threatened. If the salmon come in contact with oil, they can be poisoned and rendered useless for commercial sale.

What about future harvests?

Future harvests may be affected. Salmon deposit their eggs in summer and fall, and residents fear the sound will still be polluted. This summer's eggs will be adults in two years, and fishing interests warn of a tainted harvest.

What other dangers are there?

Ducks and sea otters were seen swimming in the sound's oil-laden water and couldn't be captured. Environmentalists say those animals likely will wash ashore dead because oil coats their fur and feathers, which are used for insulation. Because sea otters and sea lions feed on fish, environmentalists say oil spills poison the entire food chain.

What about those animals already captured? Can they be saved?

In many cases, yes. Exxon says it has brought in wildlife experts to clean the animals. The birds are cleaned by hand, using a mild detergent. It can take about five hours to clean one bird. Because their natural instinct is to return to their habitat, now polluted by oil, they're kept in small bathtubs until the cleanup is over. Other animals are cleaned the same way, but they're harder to catch. Otters often weigh 90 pounds.

— Mike McQueen

Exxon chief blames 'human failing'

Villagers say they feel 'betrayed'

By Rae Tyson
USA TODAY

VALDEZ, Alaska — For a dozen years, fishermen and oil tankers have shared the pristine waters of Prince William Sound.

Last Friday, a 150-square mile oil slick came between the two when a grounded tanker fouled the sound with its cargo of Alaskan crude oil.

"We feel like we have been betrayed," says Doris Lopez, co-owner with her husband, Tom, of a salmon fishing fleet.

But standing on Valdez's main thoroughfare of Egan Street, one sees a town that mostly has benefited from being the port terminal for the Alaskan oil pipeline. It's population has almost doubled in the past seven years.

"Before that terminal, we were just a sleepy little fishing village," says City Council member Sally McAdoo.

Built on a grid, Valdez has the prosperous village-like atmosphere of small cities in the Dakotas: one and two story buildings, neat prefabricated houses. The city recently built a new civic center and municipal building.

Only one Mercedes was spotted. Valdez's vehicle of choice: a 4-wheel drive Chevrolet pickup truck — a practical testimony to the town's average annual snowfall of 303 inches.

Residents say they enjoy the economic benefits of the pipeline but are quick to add that the region's sheer beauty is its main attraction.

As you approach Valdez by water, the city appears dwarfed by huge snow-covered mountains and glaciers.

"The beauty is awesome," says grocer Dennis Holtz.

But the isolation also has a price. There are few local restaurants and no car dealerships. Shopping means an 8-hour car trip to Anchorage.

In recent years, tourism also has emerged as an area money-maker — and it is the tourism and the fishing industries many fear will be damaged by the USA's worst oil spill.

"This could depress the economy for a large number of people, says Lopez.

In nearby Cordova — an isolated community accessible only by boat or plane — residents are worried about the threat to their main source of income: fishing.

"When the pipeline came everybody fought it, worrying that something like this would happen," says Bill Wilcox, a machinery repairman.

Southwest of Valdez — about a 40-minute ride by small plane — is Tatitlek, an isolated and self sufficient Alaskan Native village. Concern is especially high there.

"We are worried; worried about our deer; worried about our fish; worried about our seals," says Sandra Selanoff, a member of the governing Tatitlek Council.

They also are worried about a threat to their lifestyle.

"For us, it's a feeling of defeat," says Selanoff. "We have no choices. This is our way of life."

He defends way firm responded

By Rae Tyson
USA TODAY

VALDEZ, Alaska — Exxon's president Wednesday blamed the USA's worst oil spill on "human failing."

"This incident should never have happened. In my view, it was human failing that led to it," said Bill Stevens, president of Exxon USA.

Stevens arrived in Alaska Wednesday to confer with Transportation Secretary Samuel Skinner and Environmental Protection Agency chief William Reilly.

Asked if he was quizzed by Reilly and Skinner on the company's response to the spill, Stevens said "I did not feel it necessary to defend anything."

Critics say the company and its subsidiary, Exxon Shipping Company, responded too slowly to the 10.1 million gallon spill, allowing it to overtake the Prince William Sound.

Exxon Shipping officials acknowledged Wednesday they failed to deploy booms around the leaking Exxon tanker until 100 hours after it ran aground.

Also Wednesday:
▶ A harbor pilot and Coast Guard official reported they smelled alcohol on the captain's breath before and after the grounding but they felt he was competent, National Transportation Safety Board officials said.

Capt. William Hazelwood has had two convictions for drunken driving.

▶ The White House said the government would not take over cleanup efforts. Skinner told President Bush the situation was "more positive than they might have believed."

▶ Instead of protective dual bottoms previously placed on oil tankers, the Exxon Valdez and her sister ship, the Exxon Long Beach, were fitted with single hulls as an economy measure when they were built in 1986, a spokesman for the ship's builder said.

Towns bear brunt of spill

Communities near the Exxon oil spill face huge losses to their vital $150 million fishing industry because of environmental damage. Also threatened: recreational fishing, hunting and tourism in the pristine wilderness area.

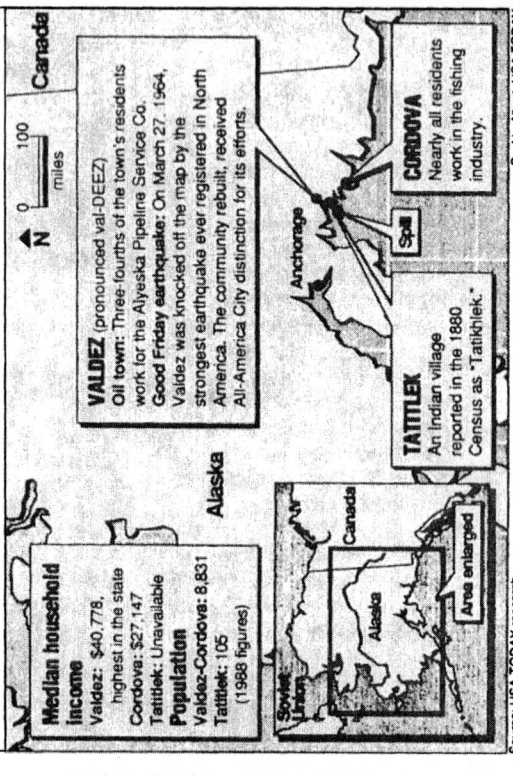

Median household income
Valdez: $40,778, highest in the state
Cordova: $27,147
Tatitlek: Unavailable

Population
Valdez-Cordova: 8,831
Tatitlek: 105
(1988 figures)

VALDEZ (pronounced val-DEEZ)
Oil town: Three-fourths of the town's residents work for the Alyeska Pipeline Service Co.
Good Friday earthquake: On March 27, 1964, Valdez was knocked off the map by the strongest earthquake ever registered in North America. The community rebuilt, received All-America City distinction for its efforts.

TATITLEK
An Indian village reported in the 1880 Census as 'Tatikhlek.'

CORDOVA
Nearly all residents work in the fishing industry.

Source: USA TODAY research
By J.L. Albert, USA TODAY

Activist in earlier spill has grim forecast

By Mike McQueen
USA TODAY

Lois Sidenberg of Santa Barbara, Calif., has a message for the residents of Valdez, Alaska:

"Things will never be the same," says the 87-year-old founder of GOO, Get Oil Out. Sidenberg started GOO, an environmental organization, after a Union Oil Co. oil platform ruptured and spewed 3 million gallons of crude onto Santa Barbara's beaches Jan. 28, 1969.

Thirty miles of beaches were coated with the sludge. Oil-soaked birds, unable to fly, died slowly in the sand. The disaster shocked the nation and gave birth to today's environmental movement.

It took two months to clear the Pacific Ocean of the sludge.

Today, Sidenberg says, the city's beaches are generally clean. But every few months she walks the beaches and sees oil.

Unocal (the new name for Union Oil) says that there are hundreds of natural oil deposits on the Pacific Ocean floor and that it suspects that's where the oil is coming from.

USA TODAY, 30 MARCH 1989

12   Oil Spill!

DISCOVERY FILE

Currents—Going with the Flow

Currents are like giant rivers of sea water flowing through the ocean. Some flow on the surface, others are hidden in the depths of the ocean. An ocean current is capable of moving far more water than the widest river on land.

The engines that power currents are the winds that whip across the ocean's surface, the earth's rotation, the sun's heat, and the gravitational attraction of the sun and moon.

The ocean and the atmosphere are like an enormous solar-powered heating system. The sun radiates energy to the ocean. This process directly results in heating, evaporation, and precipitation. Indirectly, accumulation of this energy causes the winds, which distribute heat over the earth's surface. Heat is also distributed by horizontal surface currents and deep vertical currents.

Wind-Driven Surface Currents

The wind-driven currents that flow horizontally travel along the ocean's surface. The prevailing winds are a product of planetary rather than local forces. They move in the lower part of the troposphere, the layer of air nearest the surface. Generally, they blow according to patterns and usually from a constant direction.

Although local weather conditions can cause departures from this usual pattern, understanding the typical flows should help you in your investigation.

As the wind pushes across the ocean, its friction with the water stirs up waves. Wind pushing against the faces of waves is the driving force behind surface currents. Most surface ocean currents die out at about 200 meters below the surface.

Vertical Currents

Density difference is another force driving ocean currents. Water sinks or rises according to predictable patterns, based on its density. The more dense substances sink. Cold water, being denser, sinks in warm water. Density currents are the vertical flow, rather than horizontal, of water moving from the surface to ocean bottom, and then back to the surface.

Currents Caused by Temperature Differences

Currents formed in this manner, say at earth's polar regions, move slowly across the sea floor, then rise to the surface again when they run into a land mass or converge with an oncoming current. In a colder climate, the surface water is also colder and saltier, therefore, heavier. Being heavier, these ocean waters sink to the sea floor. Spreading out over the ocean bottom, the cold waters sluggishly move toward warmer waters at the equator. Gradually, the once chilly polar waters work their way back toward the surface, replacing the surface waters that sink.

This upwelling and downwelling of water carries interesting passengers. Phytoplankton, zooplankton, and other marine life ride the currents on their world cruise. Currents also disperse plants and seeds even from one continent to another.

Currents Caused by Salinity

One of the causes of vertical currents is related to cold-water freezing in the polar regions. At the poles, as water freezes to form sea ice, the salt does not freeze with the water. As the sea ice thickens, the amount of salt left behind in the surrounding water increases. Water with more salt sinks because it is denser than the surrounding water.

At about 25° north or 25° south of the equator, a different process is increasing the salinity of the water. In tropical ocean regions water evaporates from the ocean to form clouds, the salt is left behind, the density of the remaining water increases, and the salty water sinks—adding to vertical currents.

Think about this: How does the water cycle keep the ocean from becoming extremely salty?

Tidal Currents

Tides can also be a cause of currents, but only in harbors. In the open ocean the rise and fall of the tide passes without creating a current. However, as the tide rushes into the protected waters of a harbor, a tidal current is created. The greater the tide in a harbor, the greater the tidal current. In Valdez, the water rises about 4 meters with each high tide. In San Francisco, the average tide raises the water only about 1 meter. Which harbor has a greater tidal current?

SCIENCE ACTIVITY

Ocean Currents

Purpose
To investigate how temperature differences in the ocean can cause currents.

Materials
- 2-liter soda bottle (cut off at the shoulder to make a wide-mouth container)
- One large ice cube (colored dark-blue)
- Hot water (colored red)
- Tap water
- Plastic-foam cup
- Blue- and red-colored pencils
- Unlined paper

Activity
Background: You have just signed a contract with a publisher of children's books. You are to write an explanation of how the temperature of water causes currents in the oceans. The publisher will use your explanation in an upcoming book about water on the earth to be used by first and second graders.

You decide to try an experiment that will help you visualize what happens when water with different temperatures interact.

1. Fill a 2-liter bottle about half full with tap water. Float a blue ice cube in it. Use unlined paper to sketch your observations.
2. Obtain a plastic-foam cup containing hot water with red food coloring in it. Be very careful not to spill the hot water. Slowly pour the hot water down the side of the 2-liter bottle.
3. Allow the 2-liter bottle to sit as you continue to observe. Add any changes you observe to your drawing.
4. Think about how this experiment explains the flow of ocean currents. Think about the equator and the poles.

Conclusions
Now write a simple explanation of how the temperature of water is one cause for ocean currents. Since the book is intended for use by first and second grade students, try not to use big words. You may include a diagram of the earth if you think it will help.

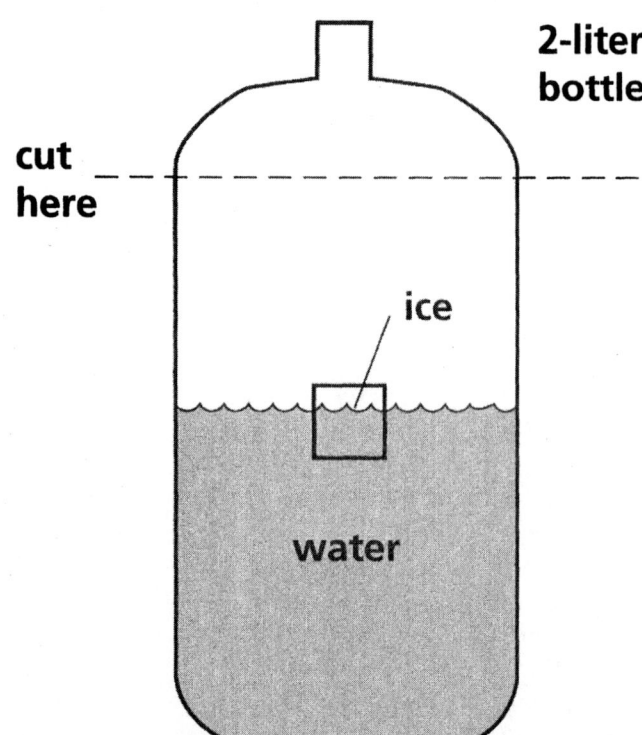
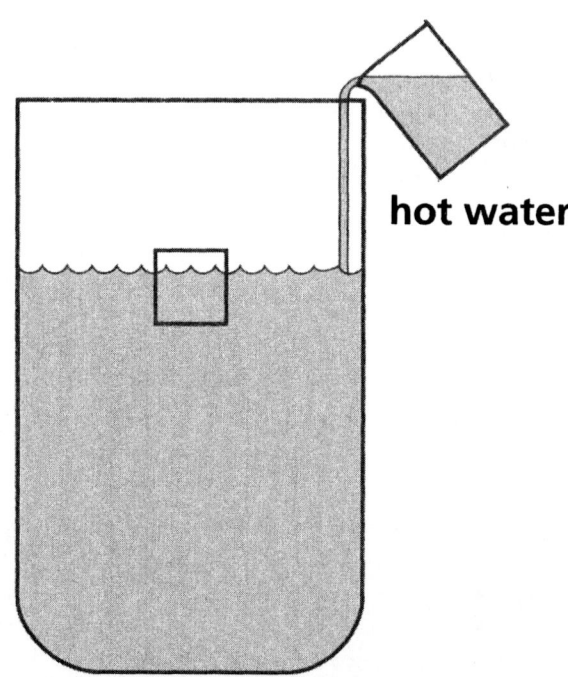

14   *Oil Spill!*

ON THE JOB

Economist

DR. DAVID SHIN
AMERICAN PETROLEUM INSTITUTE
WASHINGTON, D.C.

During my sophomore year of college, I took a course called the History of Economics; that's when I became interested in being an economist. I really liked learning about modern economic theory. I enjoyed learning about economic modeling, and I was tired of all the laboratory work in the science courses I took in my freshman year.

As an economist, I spend most of my time writing. Most of my writing involves explaining complicated ideas in simple terms so that the people who make the decisions can understand them. Good economists who are bad writers are never very successful.

My background knowledge in science is often very helpful to me. When I worked on an oil spill response project, the science knowledge I gained from the physics, chemistry, and biology courses I took in college helped me understand what the scientists were talking about.

A typical day for me depends upon whether I'm working on long-term or short-term projects. A short-term project is basically responding to requests from my executive management. Long-term projects typically consist of collecting data, running statistical analyses of the data, looking at the results, and trying to understand what implications the results have for the petroleum industry and the country in general.

The most exciting things I have done as an economist have been getting my Ph.D., teaching economics classes in college, and helping develop the Vessel Response Plan that later became part of the Oil Pollution Act of 1990. When my input actually became law, that was really exciting.

If I were on your team, investigating the economic impact of an oil terminal on a region, I would look most closely at all of the costs of complying with environmental regulations. In order to build any kind of terminal or port, you have to develop an environmental impact statement. You assume that small oil spills will happen very frequently, and if the area is environmentally sensitive (for example, it is a breeding ground for birds and fish), the cost of these frequent small spills will be high. It will also be more expensive to clean up after a major spill, if that should occur.

Some people think that if a harbor is small, spills are less costly than if a harbor is very large. But there are other factors besides sheer size that are just as important. If the oil is easily contained, the cost of cleaning up the oil is much lower. But if the oil can easily flow out to sea and

affect areas along the coastline, cleanup costs will be high. So, you can have a very small harbor with a big opening into the sea that is less desirable than a larger closed harbor.

Weather conditions are also a factor. If a big area has relatively calm weather, and the smaller port has severe weather (hurricanes, thunderstorms, and so on), that affects cost, too. A lot of wave action makes it more difficult to clean up the oil, and the wave action tends to disperse the oil. Tidal currents also help to spread an oil spill, and so a greater tide is less desirable than a small tide.

General reading of a serious nature has been a big help to me in my work. The more general knowledge you have, the better able you are to analyze new situations.

The Story—Part 2   15

Discovery File

Coriolis Force

Currents are also affected by nature putting its own spin on the matter. Traveling across the face of the ocean, currents are steered by the earth's rotation. In the northern half of the globe, currents are bent to the right; in the southern section of the earth, currents move to the left.

This influence is called the Coriolis force (or effect), named after the French scientist and engineer Gustave Gaspard de Coriolis, who discovered the phenomena in 1835. The Coriolis force, along with prevailing winds and the sun, claims the major responsibility for the ocean's circulation patterns.

The Coriolis force is least pronounced at the equator. However, due to the earth's rotation, the force increases gradually until it reaches its most apparent effect at the poles.

When water swirls down a drain, it often swirls clockwise in the northern hemisphere, and counterclockwise in the southern hemisphere. Could this also be caused by the Coriolis force?

Currents and Your Harbor
As you investigate your harbor, don't forget that if a river enters your harbor, the flow of the river will also produce a river current. Research the river's past with a focus on its history of flooding, especially major periodic flooding. Include in your presentation how major river flooding might affect the establishment of an oil terminal in your harbor.

Other currents, such as the Gulf Stream and the North Pacific Drift, may also figure in your selection of an oil terminal site. Understood in terms of the world as a whole, the ocean's major currents usually flow roughly as shown on the map below.

Major Ocean Currents of the World

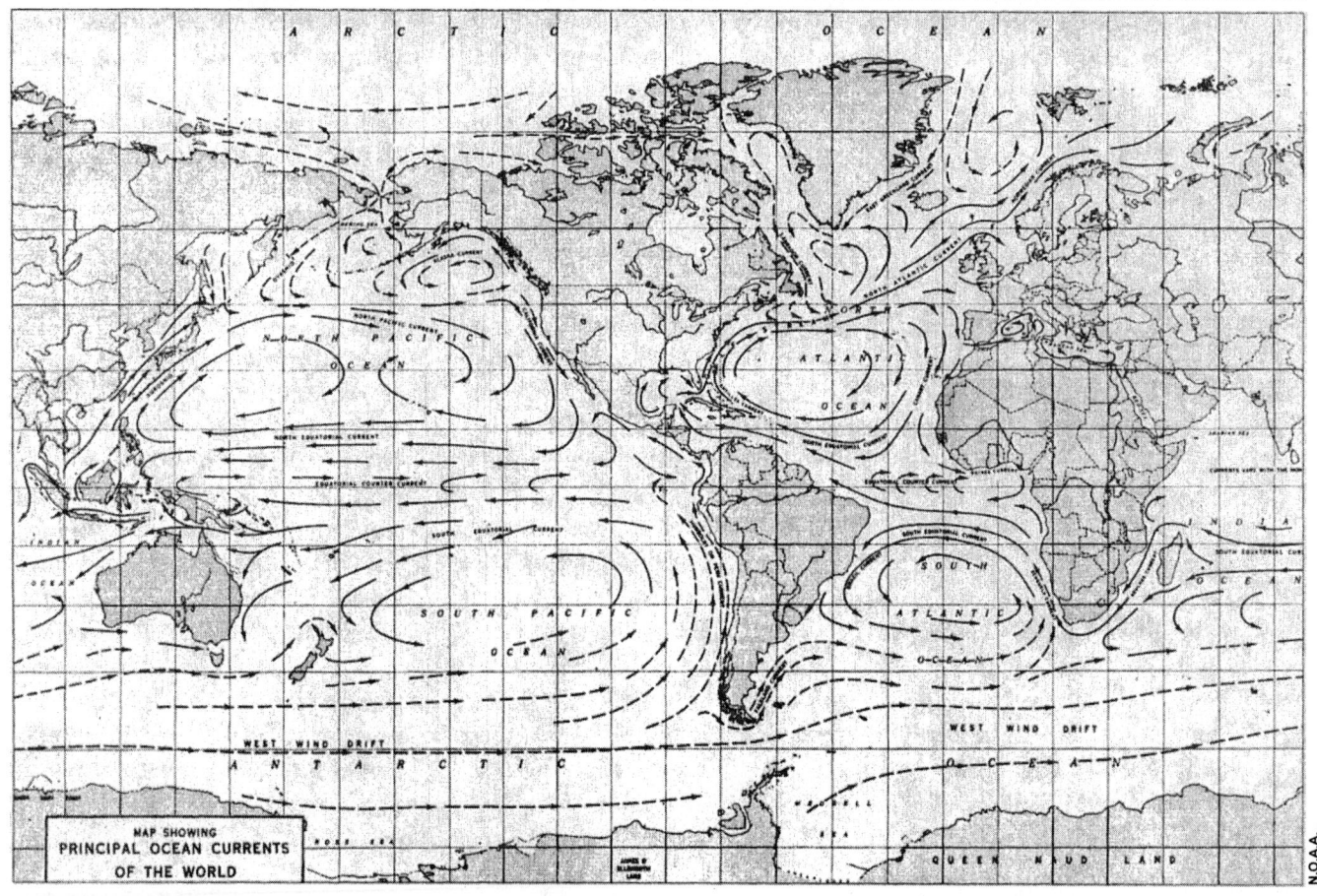

16   *Oil Spill!*

IN THE NEWS

Tanker freed from Alaska reef

By Jack Smith, AP

REFLOATED: Tugboats ease the refloated tanker Exxon Valdez from a reef where it ran aground March 24, spilling 10.1 million gallons of oil. The tanker faced a 30-mile trip to a repair site.

Coast Guard to head cleanup

Special for USA TODAY

Six tugboats nudged the tanker Exxon Valdez free Wednesday from the reef it had been impaled upon for 12 days, during which 10.1 million gallons of crude oil spilled into Alaska's Prince William Sound.

The tanker ran aground on Bligh Reef March 24, commanded by an unauthorized mate unfamiliar with the clearly charted reef while Capt. Joseph Hazelwood was in his cabin. Tests showed Hazelwood's blood-alcohol content exceeded acceptable limits.

ABC-TV reported Wednesday that federal investigators confirmed that one witness testified the Exxon Valdez was on automatic pilot aimed directly at Bligh Reef.

Investigators are trying to determine whether the captain ordered it and whether the third mate, who was in command, knew about it and tried to change course, ABC said.

Meanwhile, Alaska Gov. Steve Cowper said the Coast Guard would take over the cleanup from Exxon. He said the Coast Guard should be better able to handle coordination and management.

"Maybe that's been the problem all along. You need a military system to get things done,"
the governor said.

Refloating the tanker was a sensitive operation that could have dumped 840,000 more regallons of oil. From the reef, the tanker began a 30-mile journey to a remote cove for temporary repairs.

Exxon Shipping Co. President Frank Iarossi said the company has talked with dry docks in South Korea, Japan and Singapore about repairing the vessel.

First choice is a Portland, Ore., dry dock, Iarossi said, but Oregon officials are concerned about pollution from the ship.

USA TODAY, 6 APRIL, 1989

The Story—Part 2

THE STORY—PART 3
Assault on the Senses

Winds whipped across the Sound for hours on end. With seas kicking up and waves growing stronger, one violent storm turned an 8-mile-long oil slick into a 40-mile-long trail of destruction. Only seven days after the Exxon *Valdez* spill, oil had begun to exit Prince William Sound and enter the Gulf of Alaska. Scientists of all disciplines, including environmentalists, ecologists, biologists, and wildlife experts, converged on the sound. The assessment looked bleak by any measure.

The ugly black ooze reached pristine spots on isolated beaches far removed from work forces and the necessary equipment to implement cleanup strategies, just as species of wildlife began their migrations. The ecological devastation caused by the Exxon *Valdez* became an assault on the senses to both animals and humans.

The stench of oil filled the air. Long stretches of once beautiful beaches became littered with the carcasses of thousands of dead or dying birds, their feathers saturated with thick oil. With their oil-soaked plumage no longer capable of insulating them from the cold, birds died of hypothermia and shock. Approximately 435,000 marine birds fell victim to the oil. As many as 580 bald eagles suffered from the spill.

One bird species was especially vulnerable. Nearly 200,000 adult breeding murres, diving seabirds that look like small penguins, were killed by the spill. Those injured murre colonies may take decades to recover, if they ever do. Some now believe that the very social fabric of the murres has been destroyed. Because the spill wiped out a majority of the murre breeders, young birds now make up most of the colonies. The chicks, which now hatch too late, are unable to fly when early-winter storms strike the coast. Thousands of young murres are being blown into the sea or are unable to protect themselves from hungry predators.

Various Alaskan sites struck by oil were marine wonderlands for sea otters, sea lions, and whales. An estimated 3,500 to 5,500 sea otters alone were vulnerable targets of the manmade disaster. Like their winged colleagues, the sea otters died in droves when oil saturated their fur and made them unable to withstand the cold.

With each new tide—at one point reaching 13 feet—oily waters lapped onto once-pristine layers of compacted beach sand. Across miles of beach, rolling waves mixed and moved the oil-covered sandy sediment and covered rocks on the shoreline. The tide rolled in, the tide rolled out, and each cycle churned up the fouled sediment, creating layer upon layer of an oily sand-and-gravel mix, deep enough in some areas to touch bedrock. The natural tidal agitation also moved the menacing oil back into the water, which then re-oiled the beach.

The environmental insult from the oil spill impacted several commercial fish species: herring, pink and sockeye salmon among them.

STUDENT VOICES

For me to be involved with something so sad and large was remarkable. As for safety, twenty-four-hour tugs with booms, tanker escorts through any protected waters, double-hulled tankers, updated radar systems, and stricter laws and penalties are the best measures.

KAREN PLETNIKOFF
PALMER HIGH SCHOOL
PALMER, ALASKA

---

18   Oil Spill!

Compounding the ecological disaster, herring were swimming close to shore to lay their eggs, while young salmon were making their way out to sea. A living chain had been disrupted.

What about the human tragedy? Residents of Port Graham, Prince William Sound, and other areas in south-central Alaska were also impacted by the Exxon *Valdez* oil spill. Dependent upon such renewable natural resources such as salmon, rockfish, mussels, and clams for their survival, people who "live off the land" saw their food chain broken and their lifestyle disrupted.

In addition to the nutritional and economic effects of the oil spill on Alaskan villages—many accessible only by airplane or boat—the cultural fabric of their society was also disrupted. Young people learn survival skills and values by participating in cooperative family activities that teach them hunting, gathering, and fishing.

One native of the Alutiiq people of Prince William Sound wondered, "If the water is dead, maybe we are dead." ∎

STUDENT VOICES

Two weeks after the spill, my class went to Homer, Alaska, on the Kenai Peninsula. The major occupation in Homer is fishing. I saw how scared people were that all the fish would become sick or die from the oil, causing a loss of income for many people. During the first summer of cleanup, there was a lot of debate over the methods used to get rid of the oil. People wondered if chemicals, bacteria, or manually wiping the oil would work best. Because I had the opportunity to view many aspects of the spill, I am considering going into environmental studies or sciences as a career.

The oil resources of Alaska and the rest of the world are very valuable to everyone. Oil products are used in practically everything the world makes today. I think that the next time facilities like the Oil Terminal are built, and transportation plans are made, the developers should spend even more time perfecting the plans to prevent even the slightest leak or dribble of oil. Also, the builders should be even more conscious of the environment around them and try to protect it as best as they can.

KATIE CONWAY
COLONY HIGH
PALMER, ALASKA

The Story—Part 3

DISCOVERY FILE

Waves

Surf's Up!
Perhaps the people who know waves best are surfers. Their unique understanding of the physics of ocean waves, and their ability to exploit the surf's energy, may surpass the wave wisdom of some physics teachers. And yet it is rare to find a school that will approve taking a day off to go surfing as a legitimate science field trip.

On a surfboard out beyond the breaking waves, a surfer just bobs up and down with the water. When a wave large enough to break approaches, the surfer stands up in anticipation of the thrilling ride. As the water rushes to the beach, it moves the surfer toward the shore.

In offshore waves, the water moves up and down. As a wave passes through the water, no forward motion of water occurs unless the water is blown by the wind or carried by a current. However, when an ocean wave approaches land, it starts to drag on the bottom. This causes the water at the crest of the wave to get ahead of the dragging lower part, and the wave breaks.

Here is a way to demonstrate how ocean waves move through water. Tie a rope or string to a stationary object, or have a classmate hold one end steady. Shake the free end of the rope, and you can see the waves run along it, but the rope itself is not moving forward at all.

The *medium* is the matter or space through which a wave is traveling. When waves cause a medium, like the rope or water, to move up and down, they are called *transverse waves*.

In the case of an oil spill, if the waves are not breaking, they are not moving the floating oil, though the up and down action could helping to break up the oil.

What Causes Ocean Waves?
From small ripples to giant hurricane waves more than 30 meters high, the wind is the cause of most ocean waves. The size of a wave is determined by the wind speed, how long the wind blows, and how far it blows over the ocean.

When we observe the up and down movement in the open ocean, what is really happening is that the water particles near the surface are being lifted by the wave crest, then moved forward, down, and back again, completing a circle. Each circling motion of the upper water particles triggers a series of smaller circlings in the water particles below it.

Then, when the waves reach shallow water, the water particles circling at the lowest levels drag on the seabed. This slows the waves. Their crests crowd close together, and they pile up and break on the shore. A wave will not break until the water is less than half its wavelength deep.

Measuring Waves
If you think of waves as a series of hills and valleys, the highest point of the hill is referred to as the *crest* and the lowest point of the valley is the *trough*. Waves can be measured in a variety of ways.

Wavelength is the distance from one crest to the next crest, or one trough to the next trough. The *frequency* of a wave is the number of crests that pass a point in a second. The *amplitude*, or height of a wave, is half the distance between the crest and the trough, and is often measured in meters.

Other Wave Generators
In addition to wind, another initiator of ocean waves is the movement of the sea floor caused by an earthquake or an underwater volcano suddenly exploding. This sudden shifting of the ocean bed can produce huge waves referred to as *tsunamis* (a Japanese word meaning "storm wave"), or tidal waves, though the tide does not cause them.

Meteorites* large enough to survive the fiery journey through our atmosphere can also strike the ocean causing large waves. Since 70 percent of our planet's surface is covered by the ocean, meteorites are more likely to hit water than land.

How Harbors Provide Shelter from Waves
A harbor provides sheltered anchorage. The land surrounding a harbor absorbs the force of the waves. As it shields the harbor from the waves's energy, it is altered by erosion.

Some natural harbors also have sandbars or offshore

---

*A meteorite is a body composed of either stone or metal that originates in space, travels through our atmosphere, and falls to Earth. It can range from the size of a speck of dust to the size of a huge boulder. It could have been part of a comet or even a planet.

islands that offer additional shelter. Harbors can be artificially protected by constructing breakwaters from rocks or concrete to break the force of waves.

A port is a harbor with the appropriate equipment for loading and unloading large ships. A port is often located at the mouth of a river. The silt from the river that accumulates on the harbor floor may require frequent dredging to keep the harbor accessible to large, fully laden vessels like supertankers. A factor to keep in mind when considering a port for an oil terminal is the rate of silt buildup requiring the expense of dredging.

Predicting Storms by Watching Waves

Even long ago fishermen predicted storms by observing the waves and tides. Waves generated by storms that are thousands of kilometers away transmit signals to distant shores sometimes two to three days in advance. Abnormal tides also indicate stormy weather at sea.

The normal wave period on the Atlantic coast is about eight waves per minute, and about seven per minute on Pacific shores. The Gulf of Mexico usually experiences waves spaced about five seconds apart, or about twelve waves per minute.

You can estimate the speed of a wave by multiplying 5.6 times the number of seconds between waves. So if you observed eight waves per minute, or a wave every 7.5 seconds (60 seconds divided by 8 waves per minute), your waves would be traveling at about 42 kilometers per hour (5.6 × 7.5 = 42).

As a storm advances toward a beach, the wave period lengthens. For example, instead of ten small waves per minute, now five large waves strike the shore. The longest recorded storm swell was 22.5 seconds apart and traveled at a speed of about 126 kilometers per hour.

The actions of waves slice away sloping land and carve steep cliffs. Breakers slowly grind away the exposed rocks, forming sandy beaches. Working with currents, waves shape beaches and build up sandbars along the shore. During storms, waves also carry beach sand to new locations.

Waves possess the power to gradually transform solid masses of rock as well as humanity's creations. Waves are truly the sculptors of the shoreline.

ON THE JOB

Harbormaster

OSCAR MOLINA
GALVESTON, TEXAS

As a harbormaster, I am responsible for incoming and outgoing ships, small vessels, or any other type of boat. We handle about five hundred ships a year. I assign ships to docks depending on their length, width, and depth. Harbormasters have to know everything about their harbors. When a captain requests a berth, we have to think about tides, currents, depth, and the topography of our harbor. I have to know something about oceanography, meteorology, and navigational charts. Harbormaster is a twenty-four-hour-a-day job. I get relief on weekends, but even then I can be called at any time.

I like my job, because I meet a lot of different people from different countries. I learn something new every day. The most interesting thing I've done

is position large ships at different docks, based on their length and beam. You know immediately if you're doing the job right when you're berthing ships. It's not like parking automobiles.

I learned my job from the ex-harbormaster. He had a lot of knowledge of ships, because he came from Glasgow, Scotland.

If you are interested in being a harbormaster, you should go to a cadet school or merchant marine school.

If I were hired as a consultant to an oil company and asked to look at a harbor and say whether or not it is suitable for oil tankers, I would look at the channel. How deep is the channel at low tide? How wide is the channel? What size tankers can use the harbor? Would the harbor need to be dredged? Are there reefs or rocks that cause a hazard? I might also take a look at the potential for storms and floods in the area.

SCIENCE ACTIVITY

"When Do We Sail, Captain?"

Purpose
To use tide charts as a tool for decision making.

Materials
- Official Request for Permission to Set Sail form
- Tide chart for one month at the Port of San Fransisco (see page 24)

Activity
Background: The decision about when a large tanker can enter or leave a harbor depends on many factors (for example, the depth of the channel, the draft of the tanker, and the height of the tide). In addition, a distance of four feet must separate the bottom of the vessel from the floor of the channel. If this separation is not present, a phenomenon called "squat" can become a serious problem. "Squat" results from a force that causes a ship to ride lower in the water when it is moving than when it is standing still.

For this activity you are a ship's captain. You are going to leave harbor on the day given to you by the harbormaster, your teacher. The shipping channel in the harbor has a depth of 51 feet. Your tanker has a draft when loaded of 50 feet. This would be a problem if it were not for the tides.

Use the tide chart on page 24 to determine the time range during which your tanker will be able to safely leave. You may work together with other captains on your team, but remember that you each will be leaving on different days so your answers will be different. Record high and low tides on the grid on page 23. Connect each high tide to the next low tide and from there to the next high, and so on. Clearly mark your graph to show the beginning and end of a period of time during which it will be safe to set sail. Determine within that safe period the hour you intend to sail and mark it with a star or an asterisk.

Write a short paragraph to accompany the graph. These two parts will complete your report to the harbormaster. In your paragraph, state the planned time of departure of your tanker and the reasons you selected that time.

Using a tide table: The tides given in tide tables are measured from a level called the *mean lower low water*. This number is sometimes negative because the mean lower low water is an average of low tides, but some low tides are lower than the average. Water depths on nautical charts are also based on mean lower low water. To calculate the actual depth available to your tanker at high tide or low tide, simply add positive tide numbers to the charted depth and subtract negative numbers from the charted depth. The times are given using the military time system: 0630 means 6:30 A.M., and 1920 means 7:20 P.M.

Draft refers to the depth of water that a vessel needs in order to float.

DWT	width (ft.)	draft (ft.)	length (ft.)
20,000	72	30	590
100,000	135	50	890
200,000	165	60	1085
400,000	197	85	1215
550,000	207	95	1345

DWT stands for deadweight tonnage: the actual weight in tons required to bring a vessel down to its load line from the light condition. (U.S. Coast Guard)

Official Request for Permission to Set Sail

TIDE CHART FOR _____
(Enter the date you plan to set sail.)

Complete the graph below. Clearly indicate the beginning and end of a period of time during which it is safe to sail. Identify your requested time of departure. Attach a brief explanation for your selection of that departure time. This request must be received by the harbormaster within 24 hours of planned departure.

MOON PHASE SYMBOL: ☐

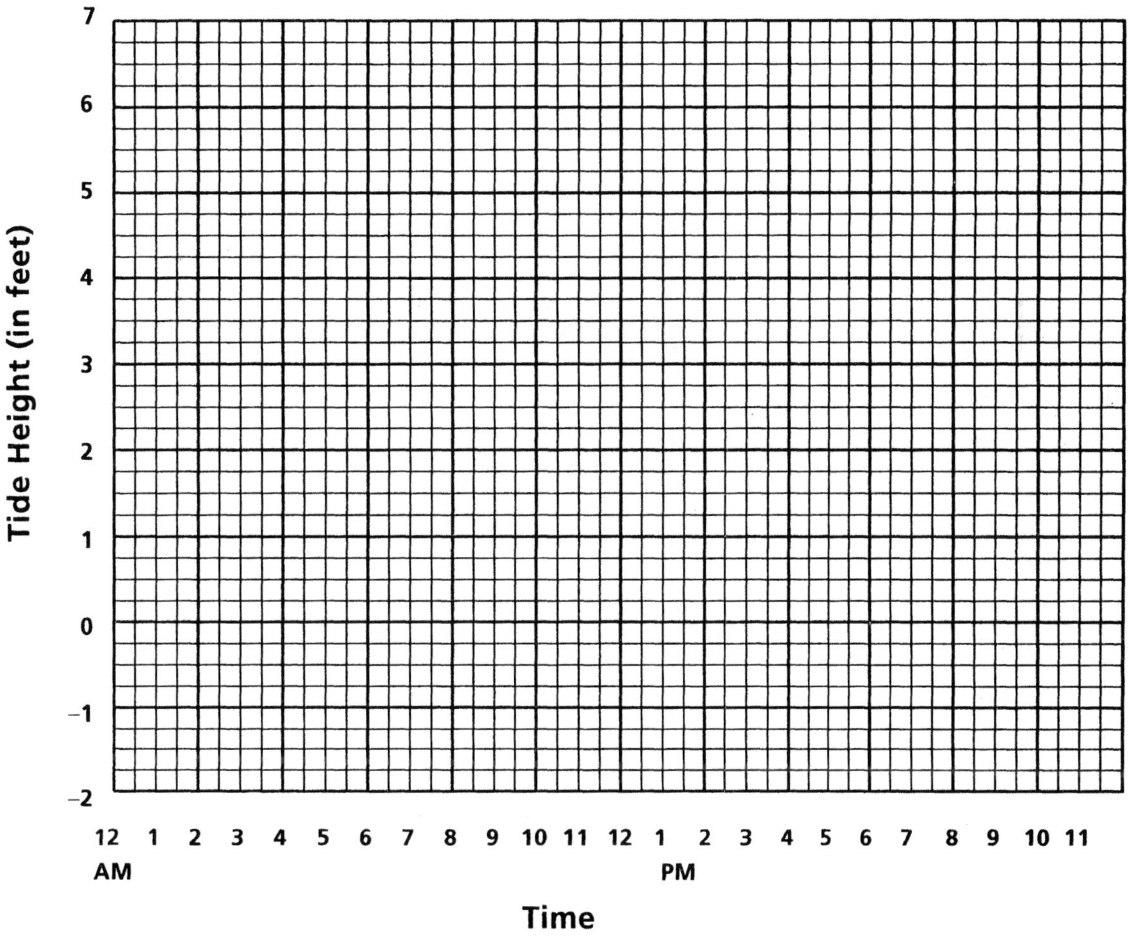

[Graph: Tide Height (in feet), y-axis from -2 to 7; Time, x-axis from 12 AM to 11 PM]

TYPE OF VESSEL _____ REQUESTED TIME OF DEPARTURE _____

CARGO _____ DRAFT _____

CHECK HERE IF AN EXPLANATION OF SELECTED DEPARTURE TIME IS ATTACHED ☐

MINIMUM DEPTH REQUIRED _____

CAPTAIN _____ _____
                (print)   (signature)

The Story—Part 3

San Francisco (Golden Gate), California
Times and Heights of High and Low Waters

October

Day	Time	Height (ft)	Height (cm)	Day	Time	Height (ft)	Height (cm)
1 F	0459	1.6	49	16 Sa	0456	1.6	49
	1126	5.5	168		1122	6.7	204
	1731	0.5	15		1746	-1.1	-34
2 Sa	0019	4.7	143	17 Su	0049	5.3	162
	0529	2.0	61		0541	2.0	61
	1152	5.5	168		1204	6.8	207
	1806	0.4	12		1835	-1.0	-30
3 Su	0101	4.6	140	18 M	0148	5.1	155
	0558	2.4	73		0630	2.5	76
	1220	5.6	171		1250	6.6	201
	1842	0.4	12		1927	-0.8	-24
4 M	0148	4.4	134	19 Tu	0253	5.0	152
	0630	2.7	82		0726	2.8	85
	1252	5.6	171		1340	6.3	192
	1924	0.5	15		2025	-0.4	-12
5 Tu	0240	4.3	131	20 W	0359	4.9	149
	0705	3.1	94		0835	3.1	94
	1328	5.5	168		1437	5.9	180
	2009	0.5	15		2125	0.0	0
6 W	0343	4.2	128	21 Th	0505	4.9	149
	0753	3.3	101		0955	3.1	94
	1413	5.4	165		1539	5.4	165
	2105	0.6	18		2231	0.3	9
7 Th	0455	4.2	128	22 F	0608	5.0	152
	0859	3.5	107		1119	2.9	88
	1509	5.3	162		1652	5.1	155
	2208	0.6	18	☽	2334	0.6	18
8 F	0601	4.3	131	23 Sa	0702	5.1	155
	1027	3.5	107		1231	2.5	76
	1618	5.2	158		1807	4.8	146
○	2313	0.5	15				
9 Sa	0656	4.6	140	24 Su	0031	0.8	24
	1148	3.1	94		0745	5.2	158
	1730	5.1	155		1327	2.0	61
					1917	4.6	140
10 Su	0013	0.4	12	25 M	0119	1.0	30
	0739	4.9	149		0821	5.4	165
	1251	2.5	76		1415	1.5	46
	1843	5.2	158		2023	4.6	140
11 M	0108	0.3	9	26 Tu	0204	1.2	37
	0815	5.2	158		0852	5.5	168
	1347	1.8	55		1458	1.0	30
	1952	5.3	162		2119	4.6	140
12 Tu	0157	0.3	9	27 W	0243	1.5	46
	0852	5.6	171		0921	5.6	171
	1437	1.0	30		1533	0.6	18
	2055	5.4	165		2209	4.6	140
13 W	0243	0.5	15	28 Th	0321	1.8	55
	0928	5.9	180		0948	5.7	174
	1523	0.2	6		1609	0.3	9
	2157	5.5	168		2255	4.6	140
14 Th	0328	0.8	24	29 F	0353	2.1	64
	1004	6.3	192		1013	5.8	177
	1611	-0.4	-12		1639	0.0	0
	2254	5.5	168		2337	4.6	140
15 F	0410	1.1	34	30 Sa	0425	2.4	73
	1043	6.6	201		1042	5.8	177
	1657	-0.9	-27		1711	-0.1	-3
●	2352	5.4	165	○			
				31 Su	0019	4.6	140
					0457	2.7	82
					1111	5.9	180
					1746	-0.2	-6

November

Day	Time	Height (ft)	Height (cm)	Day	Time	Height (ft)	Height (cm)
1 M	0103	4.6	140	16 Tu	0145	5.2	158
	0532	2.9	88		0615	2.9	88
	1142	5.9	180		1223	6.6	201
	1820	-0.2	-6		1908	-1.0	-30
2 Tu	0150	4.5	137	17 W	0240	5.1	155
	0605	3.2	98		0713	3.0	91
	1215	5.8	177		1313	6.2	189
	1900	-0.2	-6		1957	-0.6	-18
3 W	0238	4.5	137	18 Th	0334	5.1	155
	0646	3.4	104		0818	3.1	94
	1255	5.7	174		1406	5.6	171
	1944	-0.1	-3		2050	-0.1	-3
4 Th	0331	4.5	137	19 F	0429	5.1	155
	0739	3.5	107		0934	3.0	91
	1342	5.5	168		1507	5.1	155
	2032	0.0	0		2144	0.4	12
5 F	0423	4.6	140	20 Sa	0521	5.1	155
	0848	3.5	107		1053	2.8	85
	1436	5.2	158		1612	4.6	140
	2127	0.2	6	☾	2239	0.8	24
6 Sa	0514	4.8	146	21 Su	0607	5.2	158
	1010	3.2	98		1205	2.4	73
	1545	4.9	149		1728	4.2	128
	2225	0.4	12		2332	1.2	37
7 Su	0603	5.0	152	22 M	0649	5.4	165
	1130	2.7	82		1301	1.8	55
	1705	4.7	143		1851	4.0	122
	2324	0.5	15				
8 M	0646	5.3	162	23 Tu	0026	1.6	49
	1234	2.0	61		0725	5.5	168
	1825	4.6	140		1354	1.3	40
					2007	4.0	122
9 Tu	0023	0.8	24	24 W	0111	1.9	58
	0725	5.7	174		0759	5.7	174
	1330	1.1	34		1436	0.8	24
	1946	4.6	140		2112	4.1	125
10 W	0116	1.1	34	25 Th	0157	2.2	67
	0807	6.1	186		0831	5.8	177
	1422	0.3	9		1511	0.4	12
	2057	4.8	146		2206	4.3	131
11 Th	0207	1.4	43	26 F	0242	2.5	76
	0847	6.5	198		0900	6.0	183
	1511	-0.5	-15		1546	0.0	0
	2200	5.0	152		2253	4.4	134
12 F	0256	1.7	52	27 Sa	0321	2.7	82
	0929	6.8	207		0932	6.1	186
	1559	-1.0	-30		1618	-0.3	-9
	2300	5.1	155		2335	4.6	140
13 Sa	0345	2.0	61	28 Su	0357	2.9	88
	1009	7.0	213		1008	6.2	189
	1645	-1.4	-43		1653	-0.5	-15
●	2356	5.2	158	○			
14 Su	0433	2.4	73	29 M	0017	4.7	143
	1052	7.0	213		0435	3.1	94
	1731	-1.5	-46		1044	6.2	189
					1728	-0.6	-18
15 M	0051	5.2	158	30 Tu	0055	4.7	143
	0522	2.6	79		0510	3.2	98
	1138	6.9	210		1117	6.2	189
	1820	-1.3	-40		1803	-0.7	-21

December

Day	Time	Height (ft)	Height (cm)	Day	Time	Height (ft)	Height (cm)
1 W	0137	4.8	146	16 Th	0214	5.2	158
	0550	3.3	101		0655	2.9	88
	1154	6.1	186		1253	6.0	183
	1841	-0.6	-18		1929	-0.5	-15
2 Th	0216	4.8	146	17 F	0258	5.2	158
	0636	3.3	101		0753	2.9	88
	1236	5.9	180		1339	5.4	165
	1921	-0.5	-15		2011	0.0	0
3 F	0302	4.9	149	18 Sa	0340	5.2	158
	0729	3.3	101		0856	2.8	85
	1322	5.6	171		1431	4.8	146
	2006	-0.3	-9		2054	0.5	15
4 Sa	0344	5.0	152	19 Su	0422	5.3	162
	0835	3.1	94		1004	2.6	79
	1417	5.2	158		1528	4.3	131
	2053	0.0	0		2142	1.1	34
5 Su	0426	5.2	158	20 M	0501	5.3	162
	0949	2.8	85		1117	2.2	67
	1523	4.7	143		1642	3.8	116
	2145	0.4	12	☾	2229	1.6	49
6 M	0511	5.5	168	21 Tu	0542	5.4	165
	1106	2.2	67		1221	1.8	55
	1646	4.3	131		1817	3.6	110
☽	2242	0.9	27		2323	2.1	64
7 Tu	0557	5.8	177	22 W	0621	5.6	171
	1215	1.5	46		1318	1.3	40
	1819	4.1	125		1952	3.7	113
	2340	1.4	43				
8 W	0642	6.2	189	23 Th	0019	2.5	76
	1315	0.7	21		0701	5.8	177
	1947	4.2	128		1407	0.9	27
					2105	3.9	119
9 Th	0042	1.9	58	24 F	0115	2.8	85
	0727	6.6	201		0743	6.0	183
	1410	-0.1	-3		1445	0.4	12
	2103	4.4	134		2158	4.2	128
10 F	0138	2.2	67	25 Sa	0204	3.0	91
	0815	6.9	210		0821	6.1	186
	1502	-0.7	-21		1524	0.0	0
	2207	4.7	143		2244	4.4	134
11 Sa	0234	2.5	76	26 Su	0252	3.1	94
	0901	7.1	216		0901	6.3	192
	1550	-1.2	-37		1559	-0.3	-9
	2304	5.0	152		2323	4.6	140
12 Su	0329	2.7	82	27 M	0334	3.2	98
	0948	7.2	219		0940	6.4	195
	1636	-1.4	-43		1634	-0.6	-18
	2356	5.2	158				
13 M	0418	2.8	85	28 Tu	0000	4.8	146
	1034	7.1	216		0413	3.1	94
	1721	-1.4	-43		1019	6.4	195
●				○	1707	-0.8	-24
14 Tu	0042	5.2	158	29 W	0035	4.9	149
	0510	2.8	85		0453	3.1	94
	1120	6.9	210		1100	6.4	195
	1804	-1.2	-37		1745	-0.9	-27
15 W	0129	5.3	162	30 Th	0109	5.0	152
	0602	2.9	88		0536	2.9	88
	1204	6.5	198		1142	6.3	192
	1846	-0.9	-27		1821	-0.9	-27
				31 F	0144	5.1	155
					0622	2.8	85
					1224	6.0	183
					1900	-0.7	-21

Time meridian 120° W. 0000 is midnight. 1200 is noon.
Heights are referred to mean lower low water, which is the chart datum of soundings.

N.O.A.A.

24   *Oil Spill!*

DISCOVERY FILE

The Tide Rises, the Tide Falls

Anyone spending time at the edge of the sea has noticed the difference between high and low tides. About twice a day (roughly every 12 hours), the tide advances and recedes. The edge of the water at high tide may recede dramatically at low tide, exposing some bottom-dwelling animals like mussels and crabs. The up to 15-meter tide in Canada's Bay of Fundy is the greatest in the world; in some other seas in the Mediterranean, South Pacific, and Arctic, the range is never more than 60 centimeters.

The earth's tides are caused by the gravitational pull of the sun and the moon. Although the sun's mass is much greater than the moon's, the moon's closeness to the earth means its effect on the tides is more than twice that of the sun. The difference in level between high and low tides, called the range of the tides, is greatest near the time of new and full moons when the earth, sun, and moon form a straight line.

This highest high and lowest low tide is called a spring tide (although it occurs in all seasons). It's not hard to understand why the water on the side of the earth nearest the moon bulges toward the moon, since gravitational pull varies with distance. The moon pulls most strongly on the water nearest to it. Spring tides occur when the moon, sun, and earth are in a straight line.

When the moon and sun make a right angle to the earth, the more moderate tides that result are called *neap tides*. Springs give way to neaps and vice versa about every two weeks, every 14 days. Because of their interval, these tides are sometimes called fortnightly tides (*fortnight* is a British term meaning "two weeks").

As we saw earlier (page 16), the gyroscopic Coriolis force affects water in motion. This force influences tidal currents in the open ocean generally to move clockwise in the northern hemisphere and counterclockwise in the southern.

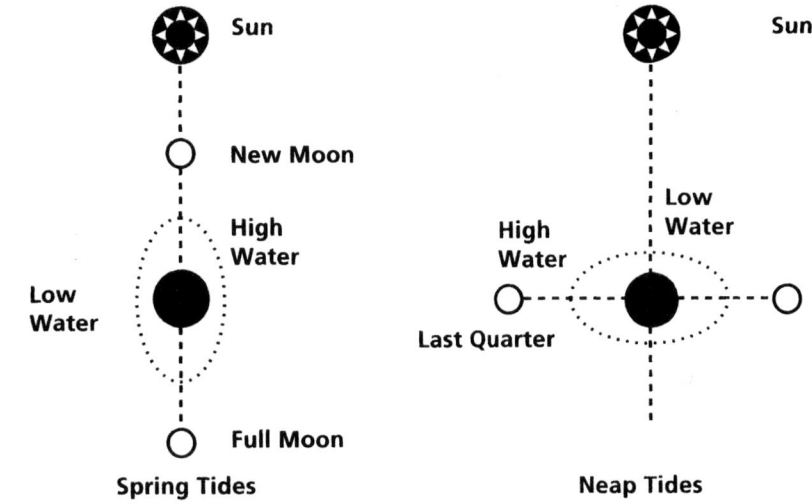

DISCOVERY FILE

The Boston Tea Party

On December 16, 1773, Boston Harbor had an unusually low "spring" tide. On that day, the earth and moon lined up perfectly with the sun. This line-up happens twice a month and causes tides called spring tides, which are the highest high and lowest low tides of the month.

On that day, over 200 years ago, the moon also reached the point in its orbit when it is closest to Earth. The increased pull of gravity due to the closeness of the moon made the 7:23 P.M. low tide so low that the water in the Boston Harbor averaged only 6 inches deep.

American patriots, facing a midnight deadline to either pay the Tea Tax or have 90,000 pounds of tea seized by customs officials, decided to throw the tea into the ocean. However, the wooden boxes landed with a thud instead of a splash, and the tea party turned into drudgery as boxes had to be opened and the tea trampled into the mud.

The unusual tidal conditions were discovered by Southwest Texas State University physicists Donald W. Olson and Russell L. Doescher. They used a computer program to recreate the sky on the night of the tea party.

The Story—Part 3   25

ON THE JOB

Marine Biologist

**Dr. Randall Davis
Department of Marine Biology, Texas A&M University**

I am a marine biologist who studies physical and chemical adaptations of marine mammals and birds. I have always had an interest in animals, but I started out studying human physiology. Then I became interested in comparing humans with other animals, and, finally, I began to focus on aquatic mammals and birds.

I was asked by the U.S. Department of the Interior and then the Exxon company to organize a rescue program for any sea otters that might become oiled as a result of the Exxon *Valdez* oil spill. I went to Alaska, built a rehabilitation center, staffed it with people, trained them, and brought in a number of professionals (veterinarians, pathologists, toxicologists) to assist. For six months we went out and captured as many animals as we could, brought them back to the center, cleaned them, cared for them, gave them veterinary care, and tried to correct the damage caused by the oil. We had a 63 percent survival rate. Then we released them back into Prince William Sound. We thought that 63 percent was pretty good. The sea otter population now seems to be back to normal.

I like my job very very much. It is never pleasant having large numbers of animals die in front of you, but working on the Exxon *Valdez* spill was a very interesting and challenging experience.

I have also done things more interesting than clean otters. I do field work in Antarctica and in the Arctic. Those are interesting and fun places to go.

If you want to be a marine biologist, take as much biology, mathematics, and chemistry as you possibly can. Don't overlook the quantitative sciences such as physics; they are important, too.

If I were part of a team investigating a port as a potential site for an oil terminal, I would look for the presence of especially sensitive areas. Wetlands and coral reefs would be greatly damaged by a large spill. They would also be damaged by the chronic pollution that results from the daily spilling of 10 to 15 gallons of oil.

DISCOVERY FILE

Ocean Life Zones

For life in the oceans of planet Earth, it all starts with the sun. Microscopic organisms called phytoplankton use sunlight, carbon dioxide, water, and minerals in the water to produce their food. We call it photosynthesis, the same process green plants on land use to manufacture their food.

Most phytoplankton (*phyto* = plant; *plankton* = drifting) are one-celled plant-like organisms that drift with the ocean currents. Phytoplankton become breakfast, lunch, and dinner for certain kinds of zooplankton (*zoo* = animal). These tiny animals, in turn, become food for other members of the zooplankton family, or for fish or other marine animals. Moving on up the food chain, these larger sea inhabitants become nourishment for humans.

Crustaceans make up about 70 percent of all zooplankton. A crustacean has a shell called an exoskeleton covering its body, and jointed legs. Tiny shrimp-like crustaceans called copepods, and krill, make a major contribution to the marine food supply.

If you peek into the world of phytoplankton and zooplankton with the aid of a powerful microscope, you might believe that indeed aliens have landed. Perhaps they arrived in a miniature spacecraft, disembarked on our shores, and jumped into the sea. However, fossil records reveal that earth was their home long before humans arrived—so perhaps we are the aliens!

These extraordinary life forms exist in all three of the sea's major life zones—the oceanic zone, the neritic zone, and the intertidal zone—although they are more abundant in the oceanic zone. Ocean life zones are determined by the variety of marine life that occupies each one. Similarly, regions on land called *biomes,* such as deserts, woodlands, tropical rain forests, and marshlands, are categorized by their landscape and the kind of vegetation they host.

Intertidal Zone

The intertidal zone encompasses the region between the low and high tide lines. Animals and plants found here include organisms that must hang on for dear life, like barnacles and marine algae, including various kelps. Other life forms spend part of their lives burrowed in the sand, like sand crabs, a common companion at the beach, and sand dollars. At low tide, tide pools reveal much of the plant and animal life found in the intertidal zone, including sea anemones and starfish. Sea birds also frequent this zone since it is rich in their favorite foods. Essential members of the food chain, both phytoplankton and zooplankton inhabit this zone as well as the other two zones.

The Neritic Zone

Stretching from the low tide line to the edge of the continental shelf, the neritic zone teems with life. The sun-warmed surface keeps temperatures fairly constant. Kelp and sea grass provide an ideal environment for this productive region. Phytoplankton and zooplankton populate this zone also.

Residents of the neritic zone include clams, oysters, jellyfish, sea worms, coral, sponges, as well as crabs, shrimp, and other members of the crustacean family.

The entire ocean is home for about 13,300 species of fish—that is three-fifths of all known fish. A vast variety of fish occupy the neritic zone, including the colorful fish found in the tropical waters around coral reefs, like angelfish and groupers. Many fish travel in more than one zone. Though sharks are seen often in the neritic zone, they sometimes come to the edge of the intertidal zone and frighten swimmers. Barracuda and blue fish, though they spend most of their time in the neritic zone, are also travelers between zones.

The Oceanic Zone

The oceanic zone stretches from the edge of one continental shelf to the next and includes the great depths of the oceans. This zone is home for the largest animals that have ever lived. Even larger than the great dinosaurs of ancient times, the blue whale can grow up to 30 meters in length. Phytoplankton and zooplankton are prolific in this zone, and krill, crustaceans from the zooplankton family, are a favorite of the baleen whales.

A variety of whales and other marine mammals, including sea otters, seals, and sea lions, are found in this zone. Numerous

▶ continued on page 28

The Story—Part 3

▶ continued from page 27

schools of fish, including salmon, herring, cod, halibut, tuna, and dolphins, also occupy this expansive region, as well as sea urchins, sea worms, sea cucumbers, and sea snails.

The oceanic zone is also home to an unusual community of deep-sea dwellers. This deep, dark region could be referred to as "beyond the twilight zone." The deeper you descend, the stranger the fish become. Some fish, like deep-sea anglers and lanternfish, have light-producing organs that help them attract prey. Large mouths and long, sharp teeth are not uncommon.

Some aquatic neighborhoods may appear to be friendly, but it is really a "dogfish-eat-dogfish" world under the sea. It's survival of the fittest and the smartest, and you've got to know the territory. Many marine animals have clever ways to protect themselves from their predators, from speed and agility to camouflage and poison-spiked fins. Fish in a large school can sometimes confuse and disorient their pursuer in the way they swim together, thus proving that there can be security in numbers.

Within each of these zones, life either floats, swims freely, or dwells on the ocean bottom. Some zooplankton spend their lives floating freely. Others spend only the early larval stages of their lives as plankton, then as adults, become strong swimmers and join other free-swimming creatures. Others settle to the sea floor, sometimes attaching themselves to it, and become members of the bottom-dwelling community. In spite of depth zoning, some of the bottom-dwellers commute 400 meters upwards each night to feed.

Recycling the Dead

The ocean operates the best recycling program on earth. Humans can't come close to its efficiency. When marine animals die, they start to sink. They don't sink far before they become tasty treats for scavenging creatures who live at lower depths.

As soon as they die, animals begin to decay. Like all other animals, marine life produces waste products. The waste products, along with dead animals that are not eaten, are broken down into mineral salts by bacteria.

Here's an interesting fact: When the *Titanic* sank in 1912 and 1,500 people drowned, some of them were still on board. Deep sea explorers thought they might find at least bones when they inspected the wreckage, but the deep ocean had completely recycled everyone's remains.

So, after bacteria are finished recycling all this life, rising currents transport the minerals to the surface, where the hungry phytoplankton select them as essential ingredients in their recipe for photosynthesis. This completes the ocean's food cycle—or food recycling program.

Numerous food chains are interwoven within this system to form complex food webs. At the same time, marine plants and animals form food pyramids. In a food pyramid enormous numbers of tiny plants nutritionally support just one top predator. For instance, 100,000 phytoplankton plants nourish 10,000 zooplankton crustaceans, which feed 1000 young herring, enough to gratify only 10 cod fish or just one porpoise.

This interdependency of marine plants and animals is essential for their survival. When a foreign intrusion, like an oil spill, disrupts these mutually dependent relationships, the consequences are far reaching and often unpredictable.

Oil floating on the water's surface can contaminate and kill the plankton as well as other life that floats or enters the sea from land or air. Although some phytoplankton have the ability to change their buoyancy, allowing them to drop below the level of the oil floating on the surface, the sunlight they require for photosynthesis would still be blocked. This alone could at least temporarily break the food chain.

As you have probably read in your studies of the *Valdez* oil spill, otters and some other animals including ducks have a special coating on their fur or their feathers that protects them from the cold northern winter waters. The water does not soak through to their skin, so the air trapped between their outer fur or feathers and their skin acts as insulation from the cold. When they became covered with crude oil, their protection was destroyed and many of them became hypothermic and actually died of the cold.

Spying on Plankton

Where currents cause seasonal upwelling of cold mineral-rich water, phytoplankton flourish. And where you find vast populations of phytoplankton, you encounter numerous schools of feasting fish. And that's just where the fishing boats would like to be.

The commercial fishing industry today uses satellite images of the ocean to locate fer-

28   *Oil Spill!*

tile fishing regions where the phytoplankton are plentiful. Since phytoplankton are oceanic drifters, their locations change.

Satellite instruments have special sensors that detect ocean color in the visible, near-infrared bands of the electromagnetic spectrum. The sensors can actually identify the green chlorophyll concentration in phytoplankton as they are busy photosynthesizing. Over time, the phytoplankton in the entire ocean can be charted.

Ocean Frontiers

Only two decades ago, oceanographers discovered hot water flowing from vents in the deep-sea floor. The vents support a flourishing population of marine life. Strange-looking creatures from the deep thrive in vent communities isolated from ocean life that depend on the phytoplankton-based food cycle.

Certain forms of bacteria serve as their primary food. The bacteria use chemicals in the hot water to grow and reproduce, in a process called chemosynthesis. Bacteria then provide the nourishment for these other organisms.

Covering 70 percent of our planet, the ocean is still a frontier. There are many regions of the oceanic zone that no one has ever explored. This vast expanse of inner space has numerous secrets in its mysterious depths waiting to be revealed.

Ocean Life Zones and Harbor Selection

What do ocean life zones have to do with your harbor selection? When considering a potential site for an oil terminal, you also need to know what sea life lives in and near your harbor. The harbor you are investigating could be a breeding ground for fish.

Where a river enters a harbor, fresh and salt water mix. This is called brackish water. A number of fish are known to like these areas, in addition to the marine life zones they normally occupy. They include herring, gobies, barracuda, and minnows. If your harbor is in a region where salmon live, salmon may pass through your harbor on their way from the ocean to their upstream breeding grounds. The young would then return to the ocean through your harbor as part of their life cycle.

Numerous other kinds of plant and animal life inhabit harbors. You need to find out who lives in your harbor, and consider what impact an oil terminal

SCIENCE ACTIVITY

Who Lives Where?

Purpose
To construct a chart of the major ocean life zones showing typical life forms found in each.

Materials
- Reference sources
- Construction paper
- Poster board
- Scissors
- Markers

Activity
Background: As experts in marine life, you and your partners have been hired to develop a chart showing the kinds of organisms that live in the three main life zones of the ocean. So many different organisms live in the ocean that it is impossible for anyone to know them all, so you and your team decide to split the task up into three parts:
1. Two of you will identify the names and characteristics of ocean life zones and prepare a large chart on poster board.
2. Remaining three members of your team will develop a list of fifteen different kinds of organisms, five for each zone, and prepare an information card for each organism. Each person should try to find a wide variety of organisms. The contract requires six things to be on each card:
   - diagram of the organism
   - name of the organism
   - type of organism (such as fish, crustacean, or algae)
   - zone in which the organism lives
   - where the organism fits into the food chain
   - whether the organism lives on the bottom, floats, or swims freely
3. When your team has finished, compile team data by placing the card for each organism in the appropriate life zone and in the appropriate position within that zone. You will have to exchange quite of bit of information in order to do this accurately. You will also have to make sure the chart is large enough to hold all the information cards.

ON THE JOB

Oceanographer

**DR. CATHERINE E. WOODY
NATIONAL OCEANIC AND
ATMOSPHERIC
ADMINISTRATION**

I am a physical oceanographer. Physical oceanographers study things like temperature, salinity, tides, ocean waves, currents, and density. We use a lot of mathematics.

I'm a "field" person. I've gone to sea for a number of years. I run field programs in water quality and environmental studies. On a typical day, I work ships. It's hard work, and it's dirty work with lots of grease. We use heavy equipment, but we have winches and pulleys to help us out. Usually the ship goes to a spot that I've marked, and I take water samples. I also take plankton samples and bottom cores and sometimes I take fish samples with a net or dredge.

Mostly, I work with electronic instruments. We send the instrument over the side and it records temperature, salinity, depth, and oxygen concentration. The instrument transmits data back to a computer on the ship for analysis. At certain depths, we also take a water sample to verify the instruments and measure nutrient levels. We do this for a week or two, twelve hours on, twelve hours off, every day. Food is very important to us when we are in the field; if we don't have good food, morale on the ship goes way down.

It's fun, if you like this kind of work. A physical oceanographer will probably never become a millionaire, but we do it because we love it. I make a good salary, but I stay in oceanography because I like doing things for the earth.

If you are interested in oceanography, get a good background in chemistry, biology, physics, and math.

If I were investigating a harbor as a possible oil terminal site, I would be most interested in the circulation patterns. What is the current like? How high are the tides? Where would oil from an oil spill end up? Would the current carry oil directly into ecologically sensitive areas or away from those areas?

30   Oil Spill!

THE STORY—PART 4

An Oily Silver Lining from Lessons Learned?

During the peak time of cleanup operations, as many as 10,000 people treated oil-stained shorelines by hand. They did this with a cold-water wash, warm-water wash, and a special technique called "bioremediation." Each treatment proved helpful, although no one method proved better than others. The intertidal zone (the area between low and high tide) and the subtidal zone (the area below low tide) each saw declines in the populations of plants and animals intruded on by the oil, but each reacted differently to later cleanup procedures.

Armed with shovels, rakes, and other devices, workers combed large expanses of beach. Hand-to-hand combat with the oil proved effective in lightly impacted areas. In many instances, an absorbent material was dabbed on shoreline rocks, as well as on the surface of the shoreline itself, to remove any telltale signs of oil contamination—a slow, tedious process. This personal attention proved important in environmentally sensitive areas where use of mechanical equipment would be undesirable.

Cold-water washing meant pumping seawater through fire hoses onto the shoreline during low tides. The technique dislodged the oil so that skimming vessels and barges with vacuum equipment could remove the oily surface water at high tide.

Considered a more effective method was the use of heated seawater to blast oil from rocks and cliffs. High pressure "steam" cleaners pumped 140-degree Fahrenheit water to dislodge oil from rock surfaces for removal by cleanup crews. However, the heat also killed any surviving marine life.

The Exxon *Valdez* oil spill prompted the first major field test of bioremediation. This method uses naturally occurring bacteria that eat oil to reduce the contamination. Fertilizer containing nitrogen and phosphorus was applied to the oil-blotched shoreline. Doing this multiplies the number of oil-eating aquatic microbes, thereby enhancing their ability to naturally consume and break down more of the oil.

Both Exxon and the U.S. Environmental Protection Agency (EPA) scientists experimented extensively with the oil-loving bacteria in Prince William Sound and were pleased with the preliminary results. But biodegradation is a natural process. Most certainly, given enough time, microorganisms can eliminate many components of oil from the environment. Still to be determined is whether bioremediation technologies can speed natural processes enough to be practical in relationship with other oil spill response technologies. This issue remains open.

It is far too soon to estimate the overall and lasting effects of the Exxon *Valdez* oil spill, the most damaging oil spill in human history, in which more birds and marine mammals were killed than in any other recorded event. In total, the oil eventually spread over some 10,000 square miles of Alaska's coastal ocean and spilled onto 1,200 miles of shoreline. Cleanup crews along beaches over a four-summer stretch of time removed approximately 31,000 tons of solid oily wastes. For over three years, the federal government, the state, and Exxon coordinated the $2.5 billion cleanup.

> **STUDENT VOICES**
>
> I don't feel that oil should be done away with by any means. I just feel that there should always be a cleanup crew following a tanker.
>
> TOMASINA DAVEY
> PALMER HIGH SCHOOL
> PALMER, ALASKA

▶ continued on page 32

▶ continued from page 31

Even though hundreds of miles of shoreline were cleaned by the summer of 1992—a laudable effort undertaken by industry and government teams, as well as private citizens—oil residues remain beneath the surface of these beaches. How this condition will impact and retard biological recovery of afflicted areas is unknown.

Disputes still rage today regarding the recovery of oil-impacted Alaskan areas. Some suggest that the environmental devastation prompted by the oil spill has been greatly exaggerated. Others contend that the damage caused by the Exxon *Valdez* disaster not only persists today but will be felt for many decades to come. In truth, there are indications of an environment on the mend. For instance, although many animals lost their lives, there was no devastation of any species.

There is no evidence that commercial fisheries were decimated, as herring and salmon catches set records in successive years following the spill. Otters, seals, eagles, and sea birds are flourishing today in those same waters that were oiled. Data gathered primarily by the government now show that the survival rate of young otters rose dramatically in 1992 and 1993.

On the other hand, one lesson learned was that the "rehabilitation" of sea otters and birds (cleansing them of oil) proved traumatic, with many animals not surviving oil-cleaning treatments. Not only was the rehabilitation treatment life-threatening, but in the case of the sea otters, expensive! Some 357 sea otters underwent the oil-cleansing treatment at a total cost of $18 million. That works out to $50,420 per otter!

Debates and controversies as to the severity and overall impact of the spill are likely to continue. Arguments and counter-arguments pit scientist against scientist from industry, government, environmental, and wildlife groups. Much work needs to be completed prior to understanding the true ecological comeback of oil-saturated areas.

In essence, the Exxon *Valdez* oil spill has created a large-scale ecological test tube, a laboratory that will, no doubt, yield productive scientific results for many years. Putting the various arguments aside, the Exxon *Valdez* incident prompts one crucial lesson to remain in the forefront: prevention is always better than cleanup.

As illustrated by the Exxon *Valdez* oil spill, technology to handle the magnitude of the disaster fell far short of expectations. Additionally, the response time of emergency teams to handle the first signs of the spill were less than adequate, with the response itself being largely uncoordinated. Perhaps more importantly, the makings of the accident can be traced back to lack of oversight of vessel movements around the Valdez port.

Exxon has been required to pay $900 million over a period of ten years, from 1991 to 2001, for natural-resource damages. In direct response to the Exxon *Valdez* oil spill, the U.S. Congress passed the Oil Pollution Act (OPA) of 1990. This public law, among its sections, requires the use of double-hull tankers, and has sparked improvements in the way oil is shipped and monitored along U.S. coasts. For

IN THE NEWS

Exxon extols spill cleanup as 'fantastic'

By Elisa Tinsley
USA TODAY

Exxon is packing up to go home Friday as a company official declared the cleanup of the Valdez oil spill "fantastic."

Cleanup chief Otto Harrison got down on his knees to examine the rocks on Green Beach, one of the areas hit hard by the 11-million-gallon spill off the coast of Alaska in March.

"This is one of the most famous beaches in the world with all the black photos," he declared. "This beach is almost as light-colored as it was.

"I love this beach," he said.

"Did he get down on the ground and kiss it?" scoffed Steve Provant, the state's on-scene coordinator in Valdez.

Provant conceded the "beach does look pretty good," but he and others worry about subsurface oil oozing up after Exxon departs.

L.J. Evans of Alaska's Department of Environmental Conservation said, "a very high proportion of the shorelines have oil under the surface."

A few places on Green Beach still had some gooey rocks, but operations manager Bill Rainey said Exxon had met its goal of making the island "environmentally stable."

"It wouldn't worry me to have my house cat run around here," he said, "except it might get eaten by a bear."

State officials said they appreciated Exxon's effort to collect the crude that spilled in Prince William Sound.

But "there are about 160,000 barrels of oil remaining," says Joe Ferguson of the DEC. "That alone would be considered a massive oil spill."

Other developments:
▶ The White House said Vice President Dan Quayle will visit Alaska next week.
▶ Alyeska Pipeline Service Co. said at least 16 tanker crew members have been stopped from boarding vessels at the Valdez oil terminal because they had been drinking.
▶ Angry environmentalists sent President Bush bags of oily rocks Wednesday to dramatize their dismay.

USA TODAY, 14 SEPTEMBER 1989

instance, the public law calls for all single-hull tankers over 5,000 gross tons to be accompanied by two escort vessels when they leave the Alyeska Terminal until they pass the Hinchinbrook entrance to the bay. It is now the procedure to have one of those escorts equipped with booms, skimmers, and absorbent material for quick response to an oil spill.

Other preventive measures sparked by the Exxon *Valdez* spill include drug and alcohol screening and testing of tanker captains and crews prior to sailing, to ensure that they are fit for duty. Increased vessel monitoring utilizing new electronic equipment has also been implemented at the Alyeska Oil Terminal. A far cry from 1989 is the quantity and quality of spill-response equipment now in residence at the Valdez port, equipment that is periodically checked to assure that it is in working order. Finally, semiannual large-scale spill exercises are now held, involving over six hundred industry and government agency personnel, making use of some fifty vessels. Given these measures and many others, it is unlikely that a repeat of the Exxon *Valdez* catastrophe can occur.

No doubt lessons learned from the Exxon *Valdez* accident will fuel lively discussion for many years to come. As devastating as the oil spill was, the *Valdez* appears to have become a catalyst for sweeping revisions of how nations should deal with oil spills. Some call the *Valdez* mishap a "teachable moment" in history. Time will tell just how many more lessons there are out there waiting to be taught. ■

IN THE NEWS
Oil-spill concerns shift beyond sound

By Tracy Walmer
USA TODAY

Oil washing up on beaches outside Alaska's Prince William Sound signals a new round of environmental problems from the tanker Exxon Valdez's March 24 spill of 10.1 million gallons of oil.

Exxon's cleanup plan approved Monday by the U.S. Coast Guard focuses on damage within the sound.

The plan "is sparse as far as what will be done outside of Prince William Sound," Roger McManus, president of the Center for Marine Conservation, said Tuesday. "That area is riddled with prime animal habitats. ... The effect could be catastrophic."

Exxon has a May 1 deadline to present a plan for areas outside the sound. Also Tuesday:

▶ Exxon Chairman Lawrence Rawl said he's confident most of the beaches would be cleaned by mid-September. "I'm not going to tell you that if you go up there a year from now you won't find some black places on some rocks."

▶ Rawl, in a *Fortune* magazine interview, admitted it was "bad judgment" for Exxon to allow a captain with a known drinking problem to command the tanker.

▶ The Interior Department announced a joint $6 million, three-year research program with the petroleum industry to develop better recovery and

By Richard Drew, AP
RAWL: Will 'make every effort' to get beaches clean

cleanup equipment and methods for large oil spills.

"We must make sure our oil spill contingency plans are thoroughly re-examined" to ensure protection of the environment, said Interior Secretary Manuel Lujan Jr.

▶ Energy Secretary James Watkins, in a Washington speech advocating oil exploration in the Arctic National Wildlife Refuge, said the spill has blackened the oil industry's image: "Every oil company will have to confront the images created by the spill."

The Defense Department has no immediate plans to send large numbers of military personnel to Valdez, *The Washington Post* reports today.

USA TODAY, 19 APRIL 1989

IN THE NEWS
Exxon says consumers to pay for spill

By Rae Tyson
USA TODAY

Exxon — after apologizing last week for the Alaskan oil spill — now says it will recover cleanup costs by boosting prices at the gas pump.

"If it gets to the consumer, that's where it gets," Don Cornett, Exxon's Alaska coordinator, said Monday. "It's just like any other normal expense of doing business." Meanwhile:

▶ Alaska's Lt. Gov. Stephen McAlpine says the Valdez spill won't discourage oil drilling in other pristine areas. "I don't think we as a nation have any other choice."

▶ Oceanic Society director Clifton Curtis — opposing proposals to drill in the Arctic National Wildlife Refuge — says the spill shows "there can be no long-term development of oil without destruction."

▶ In New York, state lawmakers and environmentalists called for a one-day boycott of Exxon products.

▶ Monday, high winds and stormy weather kept the gooey slick from Kodiak — the USA's top fishing port. Last year's catch: $166 million.

"The weather is breaking up the slick," says Coast Guard spokesman Rick Meidt.

Despite that good news, wary Kodiak fishermen fashioned homemade oil-blocking booms using logs and fishing net — with the help of televised boom-making lessons.

USA TODAY, 11 APRIL 1989

IN THE NEWS

INQUIRY

Topic: CLEANING UP THE SPILL

Stephen McAlpine, 39, a Democrat, was elected lieutenant governor of Alaska in 1982 and re-elected in 1986. Before his election, he served as mayor of Valdez, Alaska, his hometown, the site of the more than 10 million-gallon oil spill from the ship the Exxon Valdez on March 24. McAlpine was interviewed about the USA's worst oil spill and its effect on Alaska and its people by USA TODAY's Rae Tyson.

By Eliz. Mundschenk, USA TODAY
Stephen McAlpine

We're going to hold their feet to the fire

USA TODAY: As a result of the spill, will Alaska change the way it deals with oil companies?

McALPINE: We're going to hold the industry's feet to the fire to require them to do everything that is humanly possible to clean up. I warned the people of Valdez that as quickly as the media arrived and as quickly as this became a front-page issue, the media will leave and it will go off the front pages and finally out of the newspapers long before this oil is ever cleaned up.

USA TODAY: A lot of people in Alaska are outraged over the spill. Do you see this being transferred into political action that could affect the oil pipeline?

McALPINE: I think you're going to see the state of Alaska step in and say, "You had our trust. You had our absolute confidence. You defied that trust. And that confidence has been shattered. We are going to take over and we're not going to pay the cost. We're going to pass the cost of that on to you." There is a tremendous awareness and people are just totally repulsed by what has gone on. And they're going to demand that that anger be translated into some very strong political action.

USA TODAY: You saw the situation firsthand. What did you think of the initial clean-up activities?

McALPINE: There was no initial response. It was very frustrating to see what was not going on because every contingency report, every plan in place called for an initial response which would have required containment of the affected area and mechanical cleanup. The first three days were absolutely ideal conditions for that type of a response.

USA TODAY: You met with Exxon and Coast Guard officials. What did they tell you?

McALPINE: I asked them why the spill wasn't contained immediately. The Exxon official's response was that by containing that much crude oil in a very small area, the volatility of it would have created a dangerous situation.

USA TODAY: Do you agree with that reasoning?

McALPINE: Just two months ago, we had a ship come in to Port Valdez that was leaking and the response was to immediately boom the ship and, as the oil spilled out of the tanker, to engage in a mechanical cleanup. If ever there was an instance where a company turned a sow's ear into a silk purse, that was it. They turned what could have been a very ugly situation into a fairly good public relations effort.

USA TODAY: So the Valdez accident could have been treated similarly?

McALPINE: They could have got on it that first morning and mechanically removed a tremendous amount of oil. I'm not arguing that they could have got all 240,000 barrels, but they could have got a tremendous amount of it up using mechanical operations had they had the built-in capability. They were required to have that. They said they had that in their contingency report and they simply did not respond to it in that fashion.

USA TODAY: Many people have said the spill was inevitable. Do you agree?

McALPINE: It wasn't inevitable. To say it was inevitable is to say that the bombing of the Pan Am flight — the crash in Scotland — was inevitable. No one I have talked to can imagine a trained mariner putting a 980-foot vessel loaded with a million barrels of crude oil up on Bligh Reef, the most obvious hazard in all of Prince William Sound. No kid borrows his daddy's motorboat and goes fishing down the sound who isn't aware that Bligh Reef is there and the dangers that it imposes. So, to say that it's inevitable is completely off the mark.

USA TODAY: So you blame human error?

McALPINE: This involves such a calamity of human error that it's almost inconceivable that the event took place in the first place. They've got state-of-the-art tracking capability, state-of-the-art communications, state-of-the-art onboard instrumentation. It shouldn't have occurred.

USA TODAY: When the pipeline was constructed, were you in favor of it?

McALPINE: Very strongly in favor.

USA TODAY: Now there's a big debate over whether the Arctic National Wildlife Refuge should be opened for future oil exploration. What's your opinion on that?

McALPINE: We have to go forward with it. As a nation, we don't have any other choice. We have to develop domestic reserves. We have to develop other energy sources.

USA TODAY: What are the alternatives?

McALPINE: What is the alternative to our way of life is a good question. It is almost ludicrous that one-fourth of the world's population consumes three-fourths of the world's energy resources. That's gluttonous. But are we willing to stake out a political position, a social position that causes our standard of living to be dramatically reduced? I'm not sure that the American public is in that frame of mind at this point.

USA TODAY: Does the accident raise the need for tougher regulations for the crews on these tankers, or is this simply an incident of a captain who may have had some problems with alcohol?

McALPINE: I think we have to wait for the investigatory state of this to reach whatever conclusions. I don't know that tanker crews are coming in and out of Valdez drunk — of course, there have been rumors about that. Certainly, we ought to enforce the regulations that are in place.

USA TODAY: Will there be more oversight of the crews?

McALPINE: I had asked about a year ago for a person to be assigned to the terminal. Now we're probably going to see an individual assigned full time for the enforcement of the regulations. An Alyeska Pipeline Service Co. employee signs out that ship, the master of the ship presumably is there signing the papers. If that guy is drunk, someone ought to be able to say that the master of this ship is not capable of conducting this operation. That person ought to have police authority.

Oil is big business for Alaska

Alaskan oil plays a crucial role in the USA's oil production, generating 25% of the domestic production, says Joseph Lastelic of the American Petroleum Institute.

The USA produces 8 million barrels of the 17.6 million barrels of oil used per day, with Alaska providing 2 million barrels per day.

"There would be a big dent in our oil production if we didn't have Alaskan oil," says Lastelic.

"The oil industry is also vital to the Alaskan economy, generating 85% of its revenues and providing 9,000 oil-related jobs," says Maggie Moran of the Alaska Governor's Office in Washington, D.C.

Another benefit Alaskans receive from the oil industry, says Moran, is oil-revenue checks from an account funded by a percentage of oil revenues. Alaskans receive an average of $800 per year from the more than $9 billion fund.

Since the Alaskan pipeline was completed in 1977, Alaska has produced 6.8 billion barrels of oil for the USA.

— *Sonya Ramsey*

USA TODAY: Will the fish hatcheries recover from the damage caused by the spill?

McALPINE: Recover in the sense of going back to the way things were prior to the spill? No. I don't think that's humanly possible. If Alaskans had the choice of Prince William Sound in its unspoiled condition or all of the revenue or benefits that we've received from oil, Alaskans would prefer the unspoiled Sound.

Discovery File

Density and Buoyancy

You might want to float this question by your friends and family: If a pin and a ship are both made of steel, why does the pin sink and the ship float?

The ability of an object to float in water is called buoyancy. When placing an object in water, you can observe the buoyant force of the water pushing the object up and making it seem to lose weight in the fluid, if the object is lighter than the water it displaces.

The buoyancy of a ship in water, or of any object in a fluid, depends on its density. As you will demonstrate in the activity "How Much Can a Ship Carry," the density of a ship is determined by the density of the ship itself, its cargo, and the remaining air within the ship.

Over two thousand years ago the Greek scientist Archimedes was taking a bath when he suddenly figured out a use for a buoyant force. Rumor has it that Archimedes became so excited about having discovered that buoyancy could be used to measure the purity of the king's gold crown, that he jumped out of the tub and ran naked down the main street of town, yelling "Eureka!" which means "I have found it!"

Archimedes discovered that the buoyancy of any object is equal to the mass of the liquid that the object displaces, or pushes aside. This is known as Archimedes's principle.

To determine the density of a substance, we divide its mass in grams by its volume in cubic centimeters. (*Mass* is the quantity of matter in a body.)

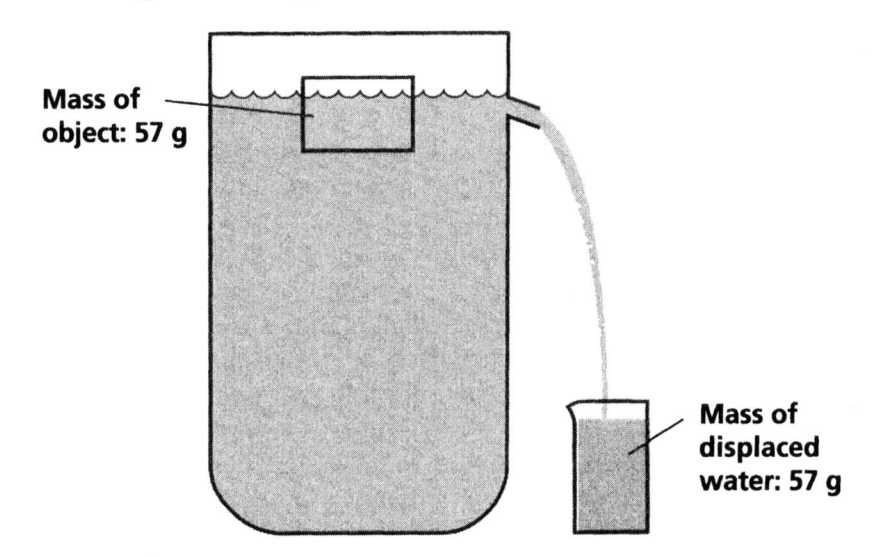

Mass of object: 57 g

Mass of displaced water: 57 g

Sea Water and Fresh Water

The density of pure fresh water is 1.00 gram per cubic centimeter. The density of sea water varies, with an average of 1.02 grams per cubic centimeter. The density of sea water is greater than the density of pure fresh water, because of the ocean's high content of salt.

Some of the variations in the density of sea water are caused by differences in salt content. Temperature can also be a factor in salinity. (See "Currents" Discovery File on page 13)

Since sea water is always more dense than fresh water, the same ship will float lower in fresh water than in sea water. The reason: It takes a larger amount of displaced fresh water to equal the weight of the ship.

So when you evaluate the suitability of a harbor as an oil terminal site, consider this: If a river enters your harbor, what effect might a sizable flow of fresh water, especially during flood conditions, have on your ships?

Buoyancy in Air

The term *buoyancy* also applies to an object that floats in a gas such as air. Common examples of airborne floaters are blimps, as well as hot-air and helium balloons, both the type you can ride in and the kind you might take to a party. Why do you think a hot-air balloon floats?

The Story—Part 4

ON THE JOB

Readiness Planner

LT. ED WIELICZKIEWICZ
UNITED STATES COAST GUARD
VALDEZ, ALASKA

When you look at the Valdez Contingency Plan (Appendix B), you will see no mention of different sea conditions. There are too many variables to include them all. We just try to state the priorities. Life is always the first priority.

I like being in the Coast Guard. It's a good job. I generally come in about 0730 (7:30 A.M.), and even if there is no oil spill reported, we patrol the harbor looking for unreported spills. We also look for vessels with safety problems. We board large tankers, like the Exxon *Valdez*, to make sure they have proper safety equipment and publications.

We work with industry on a daily basis. We issue permits for "hot work," grinding or welding around a vessel or waterfront facility. We issue permits for loading and unloading explosives and other hazardous materials. We do facility inspections, to make sure there is proper lighting and security and to make sure they have all the spill response equipment required. We also do facility inspections on passenger vessels, making sure they are in mint condition and have the proper equipment for carrying passengers. We don't want anybody to get hurt.

In the Coast Guard, we get to change post every three years. After I graduated from the Coast Guard Academy, I served on a Coast Guard cutter out of Bedford, Massachusetts. Then I lived at the long-range navigation station in Gesashi, on the island of Okinawa, several hundred miles south of Japan. From there I went to work at the Coast Guard Intelligence Coordination Center in Washington, D.C.; then on to Juneau, Alaska, where I worked as a public affairs officer for the state of Alaska. When I left Juneau, I came up here to Valdez.

I may not be a scientist, but people in my line of work need some knowledge of science. If the meteorologist isn't around, I have to know how to read weather maps so that I can determine if the weather is going to improve or get worse. I also have to read the technical literature and try to understand what various chemicals are doing, how they break up the oil, and whether they release vapors that are going to be harmful. From a biological standpoint, I have to be aware of what the product will do to individuals or wildlife in the area, and be able to read technical manuals to gather the information I need. One of the hardest things I have to do is estimate the thickness of oil that has been spilled on the water, then estimate the area that's covered. I use math to come up with an estimate of the volume of the product that has been spilled. So I guess I am part mathematician and part scientist. You might say part engineer, too.

If I were hired as a consultant and asked to judge port cities from a preparedness point of view, I would look at the logistics required for the response to a spill. We're going to have trucks coming in, and we'll need to know if there is a place to store all the equipment. How big are the airports in the area? Are we going to have to ship equipment to a major terminal and then truck it or can a plane land directly in the port we're looking at? Once we get all of the equipment in town, is there a place to store it? The people we have coming in don't go out to the field right away. They may spend almost a day or two in town. Are there places for them to eat and sleep? The logistical end is the key thing. From a logistical standpoint, Valdez doesn't score very high: It's surrounded by mountains; the roads are slippery and icy during the winter; and we have avalanches that block us off.

Oil Spill!

The size of planes that can land here is limited, and flying may be difficult due to high winds or low visibility. I am sure that these issues were taken into consideration when Valdez was selected as a terminal for the pipeline; remember, however, Valdez is the northernmost ice-free port in the United States.

If you are interested in going into the kind of work I do, be sure to take chemistry and physics in high school. Math is important too, and try to do well in English. You have to be able to communicate your ideas to people. You could have the best idea in the world, but if nobody understands you, then they're not going to use it.

In the years to come, opportunities in my field are going to be expanding because of an increased environmental awareness. People are starting to want a "greener" country.

DISCOVERY FILE

"Squat" and Bernoulli's Principle

The term "squat" accurately describes the phenomenon that occurs when a moving ship rides lower and lower in the water as it moves faster and faster. The ship actually squats! As the ship moves faster, the support provided by the water becomes less and less. This allows gravity to pull the ship down toward the harbor floor. The faster the ship moves, the deeper it is pulled. If the separation between the bottom of the ship and the floor of the harbor is too narrow, the phenomenon called "squat" can become a serious problem.

Bernoulli's Principle explains this phenomenon. Daniel Bernoulli (1700–1782) was a Swiss mathematician and scientist who discovered that if a fluid is moving in a horizontal direction, the pressure exerted by the fluid decreases as the speed of the fluid increases. The faster the fluid moves, the lower the pressure.

You can demonstrate Bernoulli's Principle by holding a small thin piece of paper under your mouth and blowing across it. The pressure of the stream of air moving across the top of the paper will be less than the pressure of the still air underneath the paper. As a result, the force on the bottom side of the paper will be greater than that on the top, and the paper will be pushed upward, or lifted.

Think about what happened to the paper and Bernoulli's law: By increasing the speed of a gas (air) or liquid (water), you lower the pressure it exerts. Imagine that instead of air blowing across the top of the paper, there is water moving under a ship as its engines propel it forward.

When a ship is not moving, the water is exerting a pressure on the bottom of the ship commonly called the buoyant force. When a ship is moving through the water, the water exerts less pressure, causing the ship to "squat." If "squat" occurs in shallow water, the ship may actually drag on the bottom. Can you explain why slowing down would solve this problem?

Bernoulli's principle can also explain how a baseball pitcher can throw a curve ball, and why the shape of an airplane wing creates the upward force called "lift." When throwing a curve ball, the pitcher causes the ball to spin fast. The effect is that the air speed is greater on one side of the ball than on the other. That difference in air pressure forces the ball to move toward the low-pressure side and pushes the ball along a curved path.

The "lift" an airplane wing creates results from its shape. Because of its shape, air speed above the wing is greater than the air speed below it. The result is that the air pressure below the wing is greater than the pressure above, and in flight the wing is pushed upward. The faster the wing moves through the air, the greater this "lift."

So, aircraft wing designers and pitchers are immersed in the physics of Bernoulli's Principle. A captain must also understand the physics of the relationship between his or her ship and the water in which it is traveling, especially when carrying oil or other potentially harmful cargo.

The Story—Part 4

Science Activity

How Much Can a Ship Carry?

Purpose
To investigate the relationship between a ship's capacity and the type of cargo being carried.

Materials
- 2-liter soda bottle
- Balance
- Scissors
- Wax-coated paper cups of various sizes
- Three 100 ml graduated cylinders
- Sand
- Salad oil
- Three different-colored pencils
- Paper towels
- Graph paper
- Metric ruler

Activity
Background: The marine engineer at Port Consultants, Inc. is on vacation and a special request has come in. A client wants to know, by the day after tomorrow, whether her ships will be able to carry the same quantity of sand or oil as they have been carrying of water. The engineer would know the answer immediately, but you and your partners decide to do a quick experiment before you send your reply.

1. Before you begin, decide how you will dispose of the used materials.
2. Remove the label from the 2-liter bottle. Cut the bottle to half its original height, but be careful not to leave sharp edges. This will leave you with a mini-fish bowl. Cut a paper cup so that it is half its original height, but still shaped like a cup. The cup will represent a ship.
3. Put water in the bottle but don't fill it all the way. Float the cup on the water. Be sure to keep the inside of the cup dry. If the cup tips or sinks, cut it down until it floats, and then dry it with paper towels. When you are sure your "ship" floats, draw a load line approximately 1 cm from the top.
4. "Maximum Carrying Capacity" is defined as the amount of material that lowers your ship to its load line. Brainstorm the measurements you might need in order to determine the maximum carrying capacity of your ship for each material.
5. Share your ideas with the class. The class should select the measurement(s) you will make. The class will also decide on a format for display of data.
6. Your task is to fill the cup/ship using sand, oil, and water until the load line is even with the water surface, and to make and record all necessary measurements. You will test the materials one at a time in a sensible order as decided by your team. Pour materials slowly and carefully.
7. Analyze the results together before you write a brief note to the client, Ms. Sharon Claggett, President, TransOcean Shipping. In your note, be sure to answer the question in complete sentences and check your spelling and grammar. Be sure to thank Ms. Claggett for using Port Consultants, Inc.

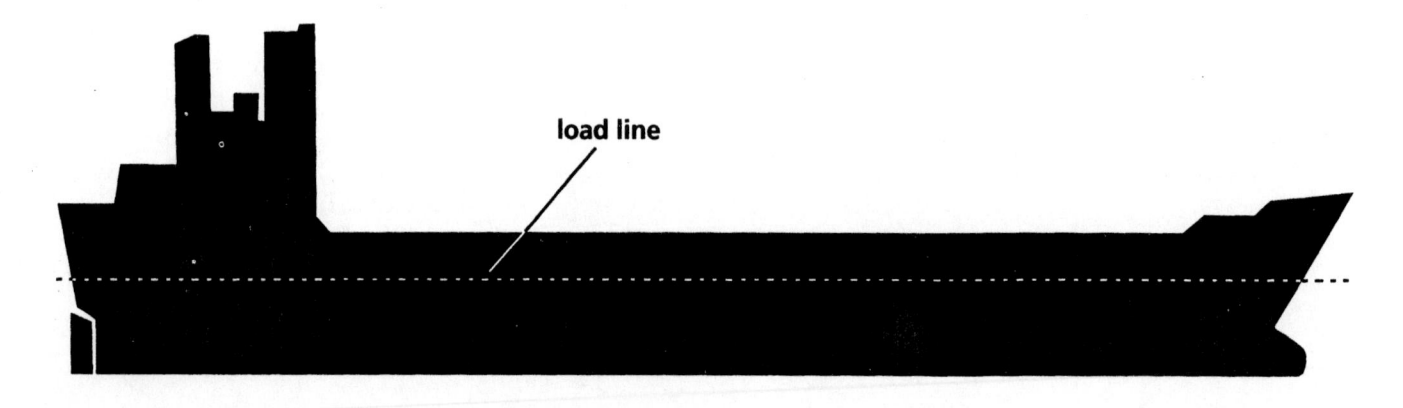

load line

Oil Spill!

SCIENCE ACTIVITY

Hands-on Harbor Profile

Purpose
To design a cost-effective method for using soundings to obtain a profile of a harbor.

Materials
- Plastic storage box (shoe-box size)
- Rocks
- Sand
- Meter stick
- Metric ruler
- Darkly colored water
- 3 sheets of graph paper

Activity
Background: Lowering a weight on the end of a chain until it hits bottom and then measuring the distance to the bottom is called a "sounding." Oceanographers often use soundings to obtain information about depth of water. Soundings can also be used to map terrain beneath the surface.

You and your team have been hired to determine the most cost-effective interval for taking soundings. The harbormaster needs a profile of the floor of the harbor. The city has received an estimate of $10,000 for making a profile with soundings every meter. The harbormaster wants to know whether information can be obtained for half the price if the soundings are taken every two meters.

You and your team will design and conduct an experiment to determine the optimum sounding interval. For the basic set-up, use the materials listed above to create a bumpy underwater floor. Then, devise a method of measuring the depth of water across the length of your storage box. Use a basic interval first, and then repeat the measurements at two and three times that interval.

The harbormaster wants both a recommendation and the supporting evidence for it. Be sure to include both data and a profile diagram for each interval. Thousands of dollars hang in the balance.

Graph your findings on three separate pieces of graph paper. How do they compare? What recommendation will you make to the harbormaster?

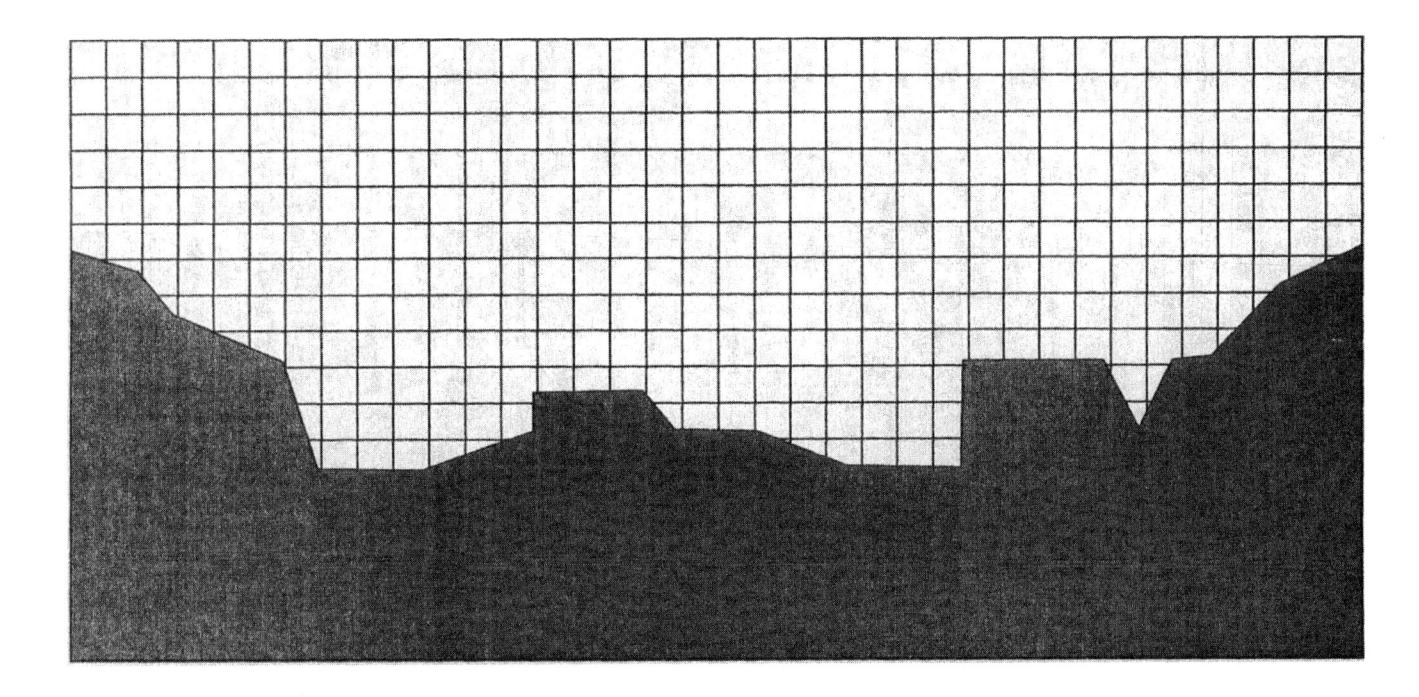

IN THE NEWS

Public angry at slow action on oil spill

Critics say the oil giant's crisis management has been ineffective

By Stuart Elliott
USA TODAY

The way John Merriam sees media coverage of the worst oil spill in U.S. history, it's "the same as if someone ran a **$173-million advertising campaign against Exxon as a polluter.**"

The chairman of the Conference on Issues and Media isn't alone in his harsh assessment of how Exxon Corp. has managed its public relations since one of Exxon's supertankers hit a rocky reef March 24 off Valdez, Alaska. Exxon's fumbled attempts to protect its corporate image have been so poor, they agree, that the USA's largest oil company is a prime candidate for the Public Relations Hall of Shame.

"Exxon. It's a word for Satan today everywhere you go," says Gerald C. Meyers, a specialist in the field of corporate crisis management and co-author of the book, *When It Hits the Fan: Managing the Nine Crises of Business.*

It's a surprising turn of events for a company widely respected as the best-managed of U.S. oil firms. It's especially startling these days, because competent corporate crisis management has become almost routine for most of the nation's big businesses.

Ever since Johnson & Johnson coped successfully with the Tylenol poisonings in 1982, two things have been expected from a company under siege. The company must do well solving the actual problem — in this case, cleaning up 10 million gallons of spilled oil. And the company must create a positive public perception of how the problem is being handled.

Among the rules of crisis management:
▶ Mobilize quickly.
▶ Involve top executives.
▶ Show concern to, and share all information with, everyone involved.

Measured against those guidelines, the experts consider Exxon to have fallen short of the standard set by Johnson & Johnson. Exxon, they charge, began fouling up almost immediately after the oil began fouling the waters of Prince William Sound. The oil giant's biggest mistake: Chairman-CEO Lawrence G. Rawl waited six days before discussing the spill — from New York. Rawl "should have been out of his chair and there (in Alaska) in flying time," says Meyers. "You get off your ... and get on the scene, and get your picture taken there. The top guy has got to take charge, step forward and say, 'I am going to personally manage this crisis.'"

Rawl's failure to follow crisis management criteria has soured everything the company has tried since then, the experts say. That includes Rawl's apologies to Alaska and the USA on TV and to Congress and a full-page ad that cost $1.8 million to run in 166 newspapers.

Can Exxon still perform salvage operations on its formerly stainless reputation? Rawl declined to be interviewed for this story, and Exxon officials won't give specifics on their plans to start rebuilding their corporate image. Experts outside the company, though, say Exxon now must:

▶ **Control its upcoming annual shareholders meeting.** This is crucial, they say. The meeting, May 18 in Parsippany, N.J., is sure to draw the white-hot spotlight of global media attention, not to mention protesters and members of the three national consumer groups urging a boycott of Exxon products. Exxon must marshal a display of whatever image and PR skills it still has. The experts recommend a special time be set aside at the meeting for Rawl to discuss the mishap. There should be assurances all resources are being devoted to the cleanup. There even should be a period for critics to ask questions and address the meeting.

▶ **Speak out more.** Until the meeting, the experts urge Rawl to send a stronger admission of guilt to customers, shareholders and government officials. He's starting to do that, appearing at press conferences including one Tuesday in New York. Rawl also appears on the cover of the *Fortune* magazine that hits newsstands Monday. The sympathetic headline: "Rawl talks of lessons learned — and what comes next." He tells *Fortune,* "From a public relations standpoint, it probably would have been better had I gone up there. In hindsight (being more visible) would have helped."

▶ **Stop saying the wrong things.** The experts are appalled that one Exxon exec told consumers they'd pay the costs of the clean-up in the form of higher gas prices. Other remarks, blaming clean-up delays on the Coast Guard and Alaskan officials, "looked like an effort to evade responsibility," says George Friesen, oil analyst for the Dean Witter Reynolds brokerage firm.

Exxon's newspaper ad was "absolutely insincere," says Meyers. "They were ill-advised to say they sent 'several hundred people' to the scene. This is a company with more than 100,000 employees."

Those botched efforts have boomeranged into a bitter backlash against Exxon. The company is joining Vice President Dan Quayle as the butt of crude jokes — and the Ayatollah Khomeini as the target of furious outrage.

Besides the boycott calls, there's a crusade developing among the USA's radio talk-show hosts — fresh from a successful campaign against a pay raise for Congress. The cry spreading along their electronic grapevine: Cut up your Exxon credit cards and mail them to Rawl. Already, 6,000 have been sent back, out of 7 million cards outstanding, Exxon says.

TV comedians are lampooning Exxon with savage skits. On *Saturday Night Live,* a parody ad for Exxon's supertanker "driving school" featured a graduate coated in oil. And newspaper cartoons showed waiters serving oil-covered fish as "blackened halibut" — and a cleaning woman who is Exxon's "contingency plan" for mopping up the mess.

Exxon's poor performance so far presents a huge disadvantage, the experts say, in trying anything else to wipe its corporate reputation clean. Earlier this week, Meyers discussed Exxon's crisis management efforts with a class he teaches at Pittsburgh's Carnegie-Mellon University. The verdict: "Exxon flunked. The crisis management is all over. Now, they have to engage in damage control."

Some think the Valdez mishap might not permanently stain Exxon's image. "I think the public recognizes Exxon is more than sorry this happened," says Herb Schmertz, the man who created high-impact PR campaigns for Exxon's rival, Mobil. "All the emphasis should be on cleaning up. The PR end of it will take care of itself."

That's what Exxon's doing, says spokesman Bill Smith: "Our people are trying to address the real-world problem of the spill, as opposed to the problem of the perception."

Certainly, the accident is "a real black eye" for Exxon, and consumers "can sympathize with the whales for a few weeks. But how long can it go on?" asks Merriam of the Conference on Issues and Media. Consumer behavior usually shows buyers' memories are short. And boycotts rarely have shown any long-term results.

If Exxon's next crisis management moves don't play in Peoria or Lubbock, the result could threaten more than just the image of Exxon.

"I believe the fallout will continue long after the physical effects are cleaned up, not just for Exxon or the oil industry, but for American industry in general. And (it will be) adversely affected for decades," says Schmertz.

USA TODAY, 21 APRIL 1989

Oil Spill!

ON THE JOB

Tanker Captain

**CAPTAIN HAROLD COUGHLIN
M.T. DELAWARE TRADER
WILMINGTON, CALIFORNIA**

As a tanker captain, my job is to get my ship, her crew, and her cargo from one port to another safely. But that is not all that captains do. I use a lot of the arts and sciences that you are learning in school.

I need to know a little about accounting since I maintain the records of the crew's wages. I also need the ability to work well with people, since I handle the crew's complaints and try to keep good public relations with charterers and contractors. When we load the tanker, I use mathematics to calculate how the cargo's weight and bulk will affect the ship. Knowledge of navigation and astronomy helps me determine where we are in the ocean and which way we should be going. Much of the equipment and machinery on board the tanker require some knowledge of electronics. I especially use electronics to send and receive messages.

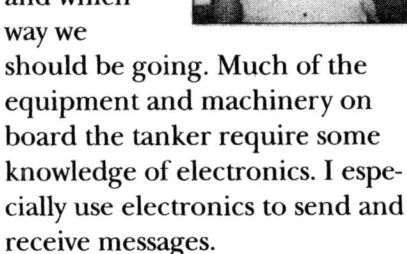

There are many dangers for a ship at sea, from too-shallow waters, to too-narrow passages, to stormy weather, just to name a few. The ship's captain has total responsibility for the safety of the ship and the welfare of the crew. I check to make sure the ship always has enough water under the keel to keep her safely afloat. My crew and I hold periodic inspections to make sure the ship is safe and able to carry her cargo.

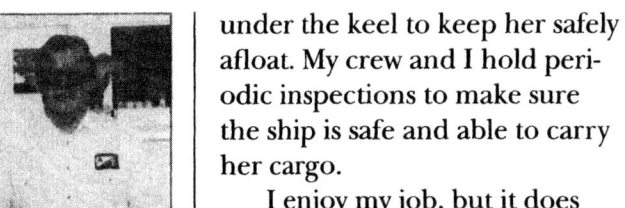

I enjoy my job, but it does have one big problem: I have to spend a lot of time away from home. In order to become a captain, I first went to a school specializing in sea navigation called the Massachusetts Maritime Academy. Then I sailed as third mate, as second mate, as chief mate, and finally as captain of a tank vessel.

I do not plan on spilling any oil, but if it should happen, we have plans ready to clean up the oil. The crew has periodic drills to practice what to do if there is an oil spill. I watch for ways to improve our performance.

STUDENT VOICES

Immediately following the spill there was little action, just shock. As the media documented the path of the spill as it swept through the sound toward Kodiak Island, there was a sense of overwhelming disbelief for most Alaskans.

The oil spill really opened my eyes to the world around me, and the two-edged sword of technology. After the spill, I became aware of all the subtle interactions that define Prince William Sound: the beaches, the wildlife and plants, the technology, and the people.

The wealth and technology we gain through petroleum does not come without a price. We must be aware of the risks and take steps to prevent crises.

WIL CARSON
SOLONY HIGH SCHOOL
PALMER, ALASKA

DISCOVERY FILE

Making Charts Where No One Has Walked or Looked

Among the many painful lessons taught by the Exxon *Valdez* oil spill is the fact that good, ocean-bottom charts cannot prevent shipwrecks. Such charts, if heeded, can reduce spills and other nautical catastrophes, however. But charting the pitch dark ocean bottom today is a greater challenge than mapping the moon was in past centuries. Clearly, land-based techniques are of limited use. Although scientists around the world are working to find out what is underneath the seas, at present adequate data are available for fewer than half the 350 million square kilometers of sea floor.

In the "Hands-on Harbor Profile" activity on page 39 you used a technique called "sounding" to make a profile of a model of your harbor floor. Sounding involves dropping a rope with an anchor from the surface to the bottom and, by measuring the length of the rope, getting a representation of the contours of the bottom of your "harbor."

The technique you used is similar to the one employed by an echo-sounding device often called *sonar*. Sonar devices record the time sound waves take to bounce off the ocean bottom in order to determine depths. Sound is a form of energy that travels through matter. In air, the waves travel at about 330 meters per second. In water, they move about four times that fast—or about 1,400 meters per second. A ship's sonar measures the time it takes for sound waves sent to the bottom (or to some other object such as a submarine) to return to the ship. This reveals the distance the waves have traveled. (See diagram.)

With sonar, a sound generator sends out a short burst of sound called a *ping*. An instrument measures the time it takes for the sound to hit bottom and bounce back to the ship. The depth is automatically recorded on a chart. Data from continuous measurements show a profile of the sea bottom along the ship's path. Through sonar and other oceanic charting devices, scientists have been able to sketch a profile of the ocean's floor.

At the eastern edge of North America is the continental shelf, which descends gently for 50 to 500 kilometers at about the rate of two meters per kilometer. Then the continental slope continues to descend, sometimes interrupted by yawning canyons, until it joins the flat expanse called the *abyssal plain*. Though fundamentally flat, this plain is interrupted occasionally by undersea volcanoes.

Eventually, a mountain range, the Mid-Atlantic Ridge, rises to reach elevations well above those of the surrounding ocean floor. Within these mountain ranges lie rift valleys where the floor of the ocean is continually spreading apart to form a new sea floor.

Your harbor soundings are not going to record mountains or trenches, but properly executed, they should reveal the harbor's undersea terrain and the hazards there.

Oil Spill!

OPTIONAL ACTIVITY

Don't Eat That Fish!

Purpose
To calculate the cumulative effect of oil within the food pyramid.

Background
How does oil enter the marine food chain? Oil and petroleum chemicals are extremely mobile compounds. They move easily through food webs and up the food pyramid. This can result in the contamination of many different species.

There are basically two ways that marine organisms take in spilled oil. The first way is through contact with oil in the water. When oily water passes over the gills of a fish, it is absorbed into its tissues. Eating something with oil in it is the second way.

Oil often starts its way through the food pyramid by being eaten by primary consumers, the tiny animals near the base of the pyramid. The zooplankton, particularly copepods, eat the oil droplets that are similar in size to algae. Some of the oil passes through the copepod and is excreted in pellets that sink to the bottom. Scientists believe that these falling fecal pellets are one of the major ways that oil reaches the bottom. Oil that is not excreted is stored in the bodies of these organisms.

The oil stored in the body fat of zooplankton is passed on to the organisms that feed on them. In turn, larger fish ingest oil by consuming the smaller fish that fed on the zooplankton. And so it goes up the food pyramid, with each larger organism ingesting the oil contained in the body fat of the organisms they consume.

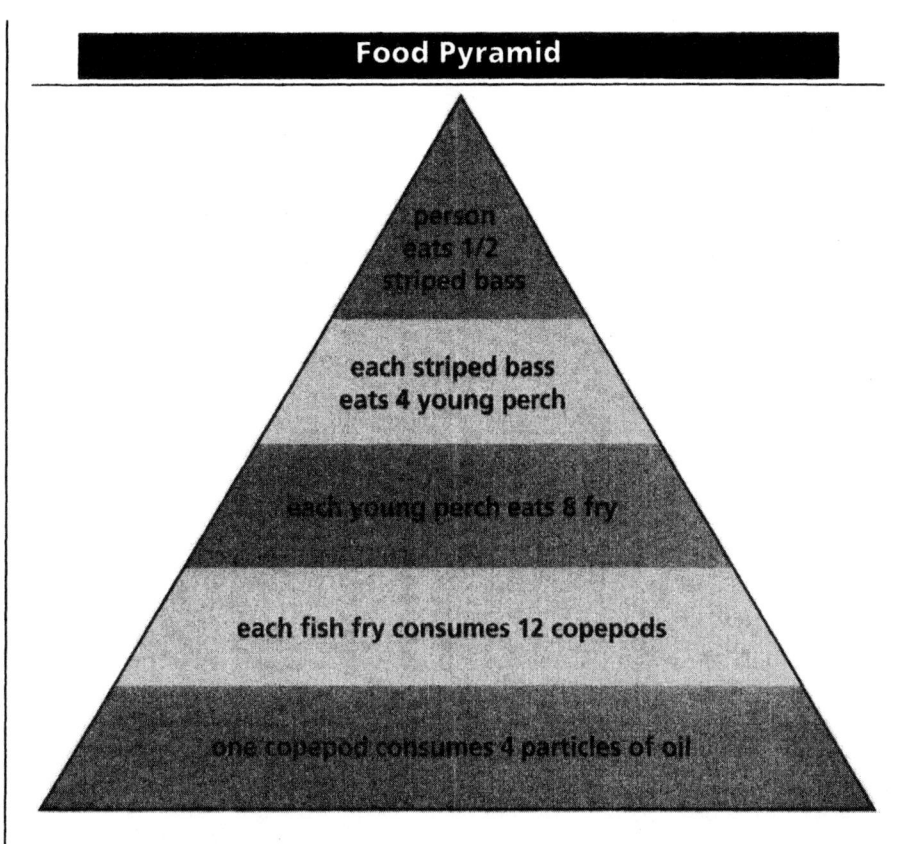

Even the oil that sank to the bottom in pellets is consumed by clams, oysters, and other bottom-dwelling organisms that in turn become a food source for the bottom-dwelling fish.

Another important idea to consider when investigating the effect of oil on the food pyramid is the rate of exposure. The sudden exposure to oil that occurs after a major oil spill doesn't usually last very long. With the help of cleanup crews, currents, waves, and evaporation, the spilled oil quickly disappears. These acute exposures usually occur in the time before an oil spill is cleaned.

If cleanup is delayed, currents are weak, and the oil stays in the vicinity of the spill, it may fall to the bottom. Once oil gets into bottom sediments, the scene is set for chronic exposure, where oil seeps out of the sediments a little at a time over a long period. Chronic exposure also occurs in lakes, streams, and rivers when used motor oil is poured down storm drains or poured directly into bodies of water. It sometimes occurs when oil seeps up from the ground naturally.

Although acute exposures tends to kill many more organisms, chronic exposure is worse. During chronic exposures, oil remains in the water and in sediments, constantly available to marine organisms. Long-term

➤ continued on page 44

Food Pyramid

- person eats 1/2 striped bass
- each striped bass eats 4 young perch
- each young perch eats 8 fry
- each fish fry consumes 12 copepods
- one copepod consumes 4 particles of oil

Optional Activities 43

▶ continued from page 43

exposure causes long-term damage to the ecosystem by reducing the ability of many fish and invertebrates to reproduce.

Materials
- Calculator
- Beans

Procedure
1. Work together with your group to design a way to solve the problem shown below.
2. Describe the procedure used for solving the problem.
3. Use your procedure to find the solution to the problem.

Problem
A person has eaten half of a striped bass that was part of an oil-contaminated food pyramid. How many particles of oil has the person consumed? Use the food pyramid on page 43 to solve the problem.

Remember, only a portion of the oil that is eaten remains in the body. Assume that all organisms in this pyramid have the ability to digest one-fourth of the oil they consume. The other three-fourths remain in their bodies.

How many particles of oil will the person have consumed when he or she eats half of the striped bass?

Questions
1. Explain why you would, or would not, eat seafood from near the top of the food chain if you knew it had been contaminated with oil.
2. How might public awareness of this contamination affect the fishing industry in the area?
3. What can be done to keep people from eating contaminated food if it were proved to be harmful to human health?
4. The oil is accumulating in this food pyramid as a result of an acute exposure to an oil spill. How might the situation be different if this pyramid resulted from a chronic exposure? What reasons can you give to support your answer?

OPTIONAL ACTIVITY

The Great Oil Spill Cleanup Contest

Purpose
To investigate different methods of cleaning up after an oil spill.

Background
Once a year, Port Consultants, Inc., has a company competition. Last year it was a donkey basketball game; the year before that it was a chili contest. No employee is ever forced to participate, but those who do always have a great time. This year, Mr. Gonzales, the president, has decided to have an oil spill cleanup contest.

If you wish to participate, you will have one week to select a method for removing oil from the water in a plastic tumbler. You may get suggestions from anywhere or anyone. On the day of the contest, you will bring the material you plan to use to the contest site. You will receive a plastic tumbler containing water contaminated with spilled oil and you will have to remove as much of the oil as you can, as fast as you can.

Procedure
Before the contest begins, decide how you will use the data you gather to select a winner. Each contestant will have a speed score measured in minutes and seconds and a cleanliness score expressed as a number between 1 and 3.

1. When the starter says go, execute your plan. When you have removed the oil to your satisfaction, record your time in minutes and seconds.
2. Your co-workers at Port Consultants, Inc. will evaluate each tumbler. They will assign a rating of "1" if the water appears clean, "2" if the water is clean but if cleanup debris is floating in the water, and "3" if the water is still oily. Remember, even the clearest water may still contain invisible contaminants that could be very harmful. So, be careful!

CREDIT: ADAPTED WITH PERMISSION FROM AN ACTIVITY DEVELOPED BY ELAINE HAMPTON, LAS CRUCES, NEW MEXICO.

Oil Spill!

INTERDISCIPLINARY ACTIVITY

Math: Estimating the Area of the Harbor

Purpose
To devise a method to estimate the surface area of a harbor and use that method to approximate the surface area of the harbor.

Materials
- Charts of the various harbors
- 1 cm transparent grid
- Balances

Procedure
Use the nautical charts in Appendix D or obtain the following maps from the National Oceanic and Atmospheric Administration (NOAA) to complete this activity. (City maps may also be used.)
- San Francisco (NOAA 18649)
- San Diego (NOAA 18773)
- Galveston (NOAA 11326)
- Pensacola (NOAA 11383)
- Charleston (NOAA 11524)
- Baltimore (NOAA 12281)

To estimate the area of your harbor you may use a 1 cm transparent grid, scissors, markers, paper, and/or balance.

There are two main methods for estimating the area of irregular surfaces. One involves counting squares while the other involves cutting and weighing. Design a procedure that uses one of these methods and use the procedure to estimate the area of your harbor.

Questions
1. If there is an oil spill in your harbor, would the area of the harbor be a factor in the attempts to clean up the oil? Explain your answer.
2. Choose several places in your harbor where an oil spill might occur. If oil spreads at a rate of 0.005 km/sec, how fast must the response time be before the oil hits the shore?
3. What other factors might influence the spread of the oil?
4. In 1980, 200,000,000 gallons of oil were discharged into the waters of the world by tankers traveling from port to port. On March, 1989, the *Valdez* spilled 10,836,000 gallons of oil into Prince William Sound. Why was the Exxon *Valdez* spill considered a disaster?

INTERDISCIPLINARY ACTIVITY

Math: Capacity of Oil Tankers

Purpose
To investigate how many gallons an oil tanker can carry and how large an oil spill it could create.

Procedure
1. Refer to the data chart of the five tankers on page 22. The capacity of each ship is listed in metric tons (tonnes). Calculate the capacity of each ship in gallons. DWT stands for deadweight tonnes. *Deadweight* is the weight required to fill a tanker.
2. If one pint of oil can produce a slick about one acre in size, how many square kilometers could be covered if each tanker lost half its capacity in an oil spill?

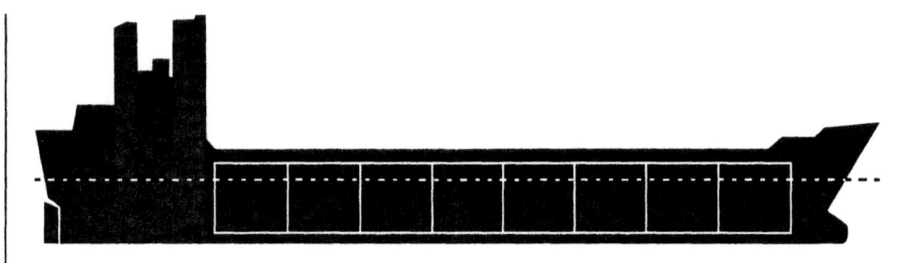

Question
How does the size of the smallest oil spill compare to the size of Rhode Island?

Interdisciplinary Activities 45

INTERDISCIPLINARY ACTIVITY

Social Studies: Is It Worth the Risk?

Purpose
You are part of an investigative team that is helping select three cities to serve as import and/or export centers for petroleum: one on the Pacific coast, one on the Gulf coast, and one on the Atlantic coast. Your team of experts is looking into the economics of each of the possible sites. Your job is to identify local industries in each proposed city that depend on having a healthy environment for their success.

Materials
- Atlas
- Economic information for possible city selections
- Blank political map of the U.S.

Procedure
Background: An oil spill may result in unforeseen damage to industries and the community. Industries that depend on a healthy environment may be especially hard hit by an oil spill. You have been asked to develop a list of vulnerable industries so that this factor can be taken into account when competing sites are compared. A site that has few industries dependent upon water resources would presumably score higher on this variable than a site where industries rely heavily on the life in and around the water.

1. As a team, take a few minutes to brainstorm a list of possible industries and natural resources that could suffer economic damage as a result of an oil spill. Place the list on two pieces of chart paper, one labeled "Natural Resources" and one labeled "Major Industries."

2. Locate and label each of the cities selected as possible sites and the states in which these cities are found.

3. As a team, review the columns titled "Natural Resources" and "Major Industries" and circle those that you agree would suffer damage due to an oil spill.

4. After careful examination by your team, select the three sites that you recommend should be eliminated from consideration because of the risk of economic damage to already well established industries that depend on the natural environment.

5. Write a team report of your findings. Include in your report any information that helps support your team's recommendations.

6. To determine the impact an oil spill can have on a local area, have team members research several of the following oil spills that have occurred since 1989:

   a. Red Sea, Saudi Arabia, April 1989, 3.9 million gallons
   b. Houston Ship Channel, June 1989, 250,000 gallons
   c. Narragansett Bay, Rhode Island, June 1989, 420,000 gallons
   d. Delaware River, Clayton, Delaware, June 1989, 300,000 gallons
   e. Atlantic Ocean, off Morocco, December 1989, 20 million gallons
   f. Atlantic Ocean, off Madeira Island, Portugal, December 1989, 7.3 million gallons
   g. New York Harbor, New York, January 1990, 567,000 gallons
   h. Pacific Coast, Off Huntington Beach, California, February 1990, 400,000 gallons

7. Include in your report suggestions for disaster preparation that might minimize the damage that an oil spill could cause to the community or the environ-ment should one of your recommended sites be selected.

8. Report your team's findings to the class.

INTERDISCIPLINARY ACTIVITY

Technology Education: Oil Spill Research and Development

Purpose
Design and construct the most efficient oil skimmer.

Materials
- Technology-lab tools, equipment, and materials
- Other materials gathered by the group

Procedure
An oil spill has just occurred and threatens a very popular resort city. You are an environmental engineer who has just developed a new, efficient means of oil collection. Officials from the resort have asked for your assistance in the collection and removal of the oil. You agree to help and must begin immediately before the huge oil slick washes ashore.

- You will construct a simple oil skimmer.
- You will work in groups of _____.
- You will experiment with various materials to determine the most efficient means of oil collection.
- Groups will complete research in _____ days.
- You may use supplied materials.
- After the skimmers are tested, each group will be given an opportunity to modify its skimmer to be more efficient.

Evaluation
The most efficient oil skimmer will be determined by the groups participating in the experiment.

PERFORMANCE ASSESSMENT

Writing to Persuade

Directions
Complete the writing activity below. Read the prompt carefully. You may refer to all your previous work in this unit.

Prompt
As a member of the firm Port Consultants, Inc., you have made your final decision on the selection of a site for an oil terminal. Make sure that your recommendation involves choosing between a pair of sites on a coast of the United States that your team did not investigate. Now you must write a persuasive report for Mr. Gonzales, president of the firm, in which you identify your choice, explain your reasons for making that choice, and persuade him to accept your decision.

Before you write, review the notes you took during team presentations. Also review the standards to be used for evaluating a site selection. Be prepared to include in your report the reasons for your opinions and the facts that support your reasons. Remember to include evidence on harbor characteristics, tides, currents, wave action, marine life, economics, and emergency preparedness.

Organize your information so that it will be logical and persuasive. Your report should show your clear understanding of the issues, should include sufficient supporting details, and should use clear, correct, persuasive language.

As you write, you should also do the following:

- First, refer to your notes on the evidence presented by the four groups on coasts other than yours. Based on this information, select one site as the location for your recommendation.

- Next use a pre-writing strategy, such as listing, webbing, or concept mapping, to organize supporting data, evidence, and logical arguments.

- Then, use these ideas to write a rough draft.

- Self-evaluate, using the rubric provided by your teacher, keeping in mind that you are writing an important business report. Then get your peers to evaluate and react, using the same rubric and also the Peer-Response Form on page 49.

- Now, revise your work, taking into consideration the responses given during the evaluation of your writing.

- Check over your work. Proofread, using the Proofreading Guidesheet on page 50, and prepare a final copy of your work.

Peer-Response Form

Directions

1. Ask your partners to listen carefully as you read your rough draft aloud.

2. Ask your partners to help you improve your writing by telling you the answers to the questions below.

3. Jot down notes about what your partners say.

   a. What did you like best about my rough draft?

   b. What did you have the hardest time understanding about my rough draft?

   c. What can you suggest that I do to improve my rough draft?

4. Exchange rough drafts with a partner. In pencil, place a check mark near any mechanical, spelling, or grammatical constructions about which you are uncertain. Return the papers and check your own. Ask your partner for clarification if you do not understand or agree with the comments on your paper. Jot down notes you want to remember when writing your revision.

Proofreading Guidesheet

1. Have you identified the assigned purpose of the writing assignment and have you accomplished that purpose?

2. Have you written on the assigned topic?

3. Have you identified the assigned form your writing should take and written accordingly?

4. Have you addressed the assigned audience in your writing?

5. Have you used sentences of different lengths and types to make your writing effective?

6. Have you chosen language carefully so the reader understands what you mean?

7. Have you done the following to make your writing clear for someone else to read:

    - used appropriate capitalization?
    - kept pronouns clear?
    - kept verb tense consistent?
    - made sure all words are spelled correctly?
    - used correct punctuation?
    - used complete sentences?
    - made all subjects and verbs agree?
    - organized your ideas into logical paragraphs?

Appendix A: Products Made from Oil

Clothing
Ink
Artificial Heart Valves
Crayons
Parachutes
Telephones
Enamel
Transparent Tape
Antiseptics
Vacuum
Deodorant
Pantyhose
Rubbing Alcohol
Carpets
Epoxy Paint
Oil Filters
Upholstery
Hearing Aids
Car Sound Insulation
Cassettes
Motorcycle Helmets
Pillows
Shower Doors
Shoes
Refrigerator Linings
Electrical Tape
Safety Glass
Shoe Polish
Plywood Adhesive
Food Preservatives
Artificial Turf
Dyes
Dentures
Roofing
Ballpoint Pens
Rubber Cement
Golf Bags
Tape Recorders
Luggage
Dashboards
Typewriter
Skis
Balloons
Model Cars

Footballs
Floor Wax
Sports Car Bodies
Tires
Dishwashing Liquids
Unbreakable Dishes
Toothbrushes
Toothpaste
Combs
Tents
Hair Curlers
Lipstick
Ice Cube Trays
Electric Blankets
Tennis Rackets
Drinking Cups
House Paint
Roller Skate Wheels
Guitar Strings
Ammonia
Eyeglasses
Ice Chests
Life Jackets
TV Cabinets
Car Battery Cases
Insect Repellent
Perfumes
Salad Bowls
Faucet Washers
Anesthetics
Cortisone
Bandages
Solvents
Beach Umbrellas
Glycerin
Nail Polish
Fan Belts
Paint Rollers
Vitamin Capsules
Refrigerants
Percolators
Paintbrushes
Fishing Lures
Insecticides

Ice Buckets
Fertilizers
Hair Coloring
Toilet Seats
Denture Adhesive
Loudspeakers
Movie Film
Fishing Boots
Candles
Water Pipes
Car Enamel
Shower Curtains
Credit Cards
Aspirin
Golf Balls
Detergents
Sunglasses
Glue
Fishing Rods
Linoleum
Plastic Wood
Soft Contact Lenses
Trash Bags
Hand Lotion
Shampoo
Shaving Cream
Awnings
Petroleum Jellies
Cameras
Antihistamines
Artificial Limbs
LP Records
Mops
Cold Cream
Boats
Nylon Rope
Caulking
Curtains
Antifreeze
Putty

Source: American Petroleum Institute

Appendix B: Oil Spill Contingency Plan

The following is excerpted from the "Substance Pollution Action Plan" of the Marine Safety Office of the United States Coast Guard in Valdez, Alaska.

102 Purpose

The purpose of this plan is to provide guidance to personnel in the event that an oil or hazardous substance discharge occurs within the COTP Prince William Sound area.

105 Definitions

Those terms not defined in this plan have the meanings as given in the NCP, RCP, OPA 90 or the Comprehensive Environmental Response, Compensation and Liability Act of 1980 (CERCLA) which are maintained as separate publications.

ACT The Federal Water Pollution Control Act, as amended.

API GRAVITY An empirical scale for measuring the viscosity of liquid petroleum products, the unit being called the "degree API". Generally the lower the API gravity the higher the viscosity.

ASH Inorganic residue remaining after ignition of combustible substances determined by definite prescribed methods.

ASPHALTS Black, solid or semisolid bitumens which occur in nature or are obtained as residues during petroleum refining.

BOILING POINT The temperature at which the vapor pressure of a liquid is equal to the pressure of the atmosphere.

BUNKER "C" OIL A general term for heavy oils used as fuel on ships and in industry. It often refers to No. 5 and 6 fuel oils.

BUNKERING The process of fueling a ship.

COASTAL ZONE All U.S. waters subject to the tide, U.S. waters of the Great Lakes, specified ports on the inland rivers, waters of the contiguous zone, other waters of the high seas subject to the NCP, and the land surface or land substrata, ground waters, and ambient air proximal to those waters. The term *coastal zone* delineates an area of federal responsibility for response action. Precise boundaries are determined by EPA/USCG agreements and identified in federal regional contingency plans. All waters within the COTP Prince William Sound's area of responsibility are coastal.

CONTIGUOUS ZONE The entire zone established or to be established by the United States under Article 24 of the Convention of the Territorial Sea and the Contiguous Zone, which is contiguous to the territorial sea and which extends nine miles seaward from the outer limit of the territorial sea.

DEMULSIBILITY The resistance of an oil to emulsify, or the ability of an oil to separate from any water with which it is mixed. The better the demulsibility rating, the more quickly the oil separates from water.

DENSITY Density is the term meaning the mass of a unit volume. Its numerical expression varies with the units selected.

DISCHARGE Includes, but is not limited to, any spilling, leaking, pouring, emitting, emptying, or dumping of oil. For the purposes of the NCP, discharge shall also mean a substantial threat of a discharge.

EMULSION A mechanical mixture of two liquids which do not naturally mix, as oil and water. Water-in-oil emulsions have water as the external phase and the internal phase is oil.

FIRE POINT The lowest temperature at which a substance vaporizes rapidly enough to burn for at least 5 seconds after ignition, under standard conditions.

FLASH POINT The lowest temperature at which a substance gives off sufficient vapor to form a mixture which will ignite, when exposed to an ignition source, under standard conditions.

FRACTION Refinery term for a product of fractional distillation having a restricted boiling range.

FUEL OIL GRADE Numerical ratings ranging from 1 to 6. The lower the grade number, the thinner the oil is and the more easily it evaporates. A high number indicates a relatively thick, heavy oil. No. 1 and 2 fuel oils are usually used in domestic heaters, and the others are used by industry and ships. At low temperatures No. 5 and 6 oils are solids which must be liquefied by heating. Kerosenes, coal oil, and range oil are all No. 1 oils.

HAZARDOUS SUBSTANCE An element or compound, other than oil, which presents an imminent or substantial threat to the public health or welfare. For a precise definition, see the NCP.

INLAND ZONE The environment inland of the coastal zone excluding the Great Lakes and specified ports and harbors of inland rivers. The term *inland zone* delineates the area of Federal responsibility for response action. Precise boundaries are determined by EPA/USCG agreement and identified in Federal regional contingency plans.

INNAGE Space occupied in a product container.

IN PERSONAM An action "in personam" is instituted against an individual, usually through the personal service of process, and may result in imposition of a liability directly upon the person of a defendant.

IN REM An action "in rem" is one in which the vessel or thing itself is treated as offender and made defendant without any proceeding against the owners or even mentioning their names.

The decree in an action in rem is enforced directly against the rem by condemnation and sale thereof.

LOAD ON TOP A procedure for ballasting and cleaning unloaded tankers without discharging oil. Half of the tanks are first filled with seawater while the others are cleaned by washing. Then oil from the cleaned tanks, along with oil which has separated out in the full tanks, is pumped into a single slop tank. The clean water in the full tanks is then discharged while the freshly cleaned tanks are filled with seawater. Ballast is thus constantly maintained.

MAJOR DISASTER Any hurricane, tornado, storm, flood, high water, wind-driven water, tidal wave, earthquake, drought, fire, or other catastrophe in any part of the United States which, in the determination of the president, is or threatens to become of sufficient severity and magnitude to warrant disaster assistance by the federal government. This federal assistance supplements the efforts and available resources of State and local governments and relief organizations in alleviating the damage, loss, hardship or suffering caused.

MAJOR SPILL A discharge of oil of more than 10,000 gallons in inland waters or more than 100,000 gallons in coastal waters.

MEDIUM SPILL A discharge of oil of 1,000 gallons to 10,000 gallons in inland waters or 10,000 gallons to 100,000 gallons in coastal waters.

MINOR SPILL A discharge of oil of less than 1,000 gallons in inland waters, or less than 10,000 gallons in coastal waters.

OIL Oil of any kind or in any form including, but not limited to, petroleum fuel oil, sludge, oil refuse, and oil mixed with wastes other than dredged spoil.

OUTAGE Space left in a product container to allow for expansion during temperature changes it may undergo during shipment and use. Measurement or space not occupied.

pH Term used to express the apparent acidity or alkalinity of aqueous solutions; values below 7 indicate acid solutions and values above 7 indicate alkaline solutions.

POUR POINT The lowest temperature at which an oil will flow or can be poured under specified conditions of test.

REMOVE OR REMOVAL See the NCP for precise definition.

SCUPPERS Openings around the deck of a vessel which allow water falling onto the deck to flow overboard. Should be plugged during fuel transfer.

SHEEN An iridescent appearance on the surface of water.

SLUDGE OIL Muddy impurities and acid which have settled from a mineral oil.

SPECIFIC GRAVITY The ratio of the weight of a given volume of the material at a stated temperature to the weight of an equal volume of distilled water at the same temperature.

SPONTANEOUS IGNITION TEMPERATURE (S.I.T.) The temperature at which an oil ignites of its own accord in the presence of air or oxygen under standard conditions.

Appendix B

TONNAGE There are various tonnages applied to merchant ships. The one commonly implied is gross tonnage although, in these days, tankers and other bulk-carriers are often referred to in terms of deadweight.

Gross tonnage 100 cubic feet of permanently enclosed space is equal to one gross ton. It has nothing whatever to do with weight. This is usually the registered tonnage although it may vary somewhat according to the classifying authority nationality.

Net tonnage The earning capacity of a ship. The gross tonnage after deduction of certain spaces, such as engine and boiler rooms, crew accommodation, stores, equipment, etc. Port and harbor dues are based on this tonnage.

Displacement tonnage The actual weight in long tons, varying according to whether a vessel is in light or loaded condition. War ships are always spoken of by this form of measurement.

Deadweight tonnage The actual weight in tons of cargo stores, etc., required to bring a vessel down to her load line, from the light condition. Cargo deadweight is, as its name implies, the actual weight in tons of the cargo when loaded, as distinct from stores, ballast, etc.

ULLAGE The amount by which a tank or vessel lacks being filled.

VISCOSITY The property of liquids which causes them to resist instantaneous rearrangement of their parts due to internal friction. The resistance which the particles of a liquid offer to a force tending to move them in relation to each other. Viscosity of oils is usually expressed as the number of seconds at a definite temperature required for a standard quantity of oil to flow through a standard apparatus.

VISCOUS Thick, resistant to flow, having a high viscosity.

VOLATILE The ability of a liquid to readily vaporize.

WATERS OF THE UNITED STATES As defined in 33 CFR 2.05–25(b)1 & 2.

301 Traffic Patterns

The majority of the petroleum products handled transit by way of the Prince William sound Vessel Traffic Separation Scheme which leads through Hinchinbrook Entrance to Port Valdez. Coastal and seagoing tankers may transit through Montague Strait when coming from Cook Inlet ports or Kodiak Island. Routes to Whittier and Cordova also use these entrances to the sound.

302 Facilities

There are numerous petroleum transfer facilities and two container terminals within COTP Prince William Sound's area of responsibility. The major ones are described below.

a. Alyeska Trans-Alaskan Pipeline Terminal, also called the Alyeska Marine Terminal, is located on the south shore of Port Valdez approximately 2.25 miles, by water, from the city of Valdez. It is a transfer and storage facility consisting of four berths with four loading arms on each berth. There are eighteen storage tanks with a total capacity of approximately 10 million barrels.

b. Tesoro-Alaskan Petroleum is located on Mineral Creek Loop Road approximately 2.25 miles east of the city of Valdez. It is a transfer and storage facility consisting of two transfer lines and two tanks with a capacity of 40,000 barrels of product. While not an active marine oil transfer facility, the proximity of the tanks to the water makes them noteworthy for planning purposes.

c. A second Tesoro-Alaskan facility is located on the north shore of Port Valdez between the small boat harbor and the city dock. It is a transfer and storage facility consisting of seven transfer lines and sixteen tanks with a total capacity of 164,074 barrels.

d. Orca Oil Co. is located on the southeastern shore of Orca Inlet approximately 1 mile north of the town of Cordova. It is a transfer and storage facility consisting of four transfer lines and nine tanks with a total capacity of 55,917 barrels of product.

e. The port of Valdez Container Terminal is located off of Mineral Creek Loop Road approximately 1.5 miles east of the city of Valdez.

f. The Cordova Container Terminal is located at the Cordova City Dock adjacent to the Orca Oil facility.

304 Geography

304.1 Prince William Sound.
It is an extensive body of water with an area of about 2,500 square miles. It is very irregular in outline with approximately 3,500 miles of shoreline. The entrance, from Cape Puget to Point Whitshed, is 58 miles across, but is protected by series of islands. They are Montague, Hinchinbrook, and Hawkins Islands. Many of the islands and peninsulas within the sound are tree covered with rocky and sometimes precipitous shorelines. Behind those are the Chugach and Kenai mountains, which rise to heights greater than 13,000 feet.

304.2 Port Valdez.
Port Valdez is a body of water approximately 12 miles long and 2.5 miles wide located in northeast Prince William Sound. It is a natural deep-water fjord and the most northerly ice free port in Alaska. From Port Valdez, water routes proceed southwest through the Valdez Narrows, to the Valdez Arm and into Prince William Sound. Port Valdez is virtually surrounded by mountains. Only the entrance through the Narrows and Lowe River area at the east end of the port provide a break. The shoreline is dominated by steeply inclined rock walls with occasional sloping, rocky beaches and gravelly deltas. Extensive sand-silt-rock tidal flats are found east of Valdez at the Lowe River and Mineral Creek Mouths. Also the Robe River and numerous creeks flow into Port Valdez. The fjord that is Port Valdez has a shallow sill about 390 feet deep at the south end of Narrows. A second sill, 460 feet deep, lies midway in the Narrows. The Port itself has a maximum depth of 810 feet and an average depth of 675 feet. Tidal currents within the port are not strong, generally less than .75 knots. Wind-driven currents dominate surface movement during high-wind periods and waves rarely exceed 3 feet.

304.3 Orca Inlet.
Orca Inlet is located in the lower portion of Prince William Sound. The city of Cordova sits on the east side of Orca Inlet. The most prominent features are Mount Eyak and Mount Eccles which are directly above the town. Due to the earthquake in 1964 as much as 6.3 feet uplift was experienced in Orca Inlet. The average flood tide is approximately 1.8 knots and 1.0 knots ebb.

304.4 Shoreline.
The land in Prince William Sound can be divided into three categories: private, public, or native. In order to insure that we are not violating any areas of historical or archeological significance, we should determine the general ownership of the land before beginning cleanup actions. The National Park Service and Bureau of Indian Affairs also have information on locations of historical or archaeological significance.

305 Vulnerable Areas
Information concerning the environmentally sensitive areas of Prince William and Port Valdez is contained in a sensitivity atlas, which is available at MSO Valdez, that displays regions by season and type of resource.

307 Dispersant Use Guidelines
Pre-approved dispersant use guidelines exist for the Prince William sound area. They are included in the Regional Contingency Plan located in the OSC Pollution Response Library.

308 Worst Case Scenario
The worst case scenario is a foreign registered, ultra-large crude carrier which grounds in the vicinity of Point Freemantle in late winter. Tanker passage would take place during a late-afternoon snowstorm which would prevent the OSC from making a full appraisal of the situation for at least 14 hours. An initial release of at least 180,000 barrels could be anticipated in the first eight hours. An additional catastrophic release could be expected if the tanker were to break up. Weather and avalanche conditions have closed Thompson Pass for a minimum of 24 hours, with a real possibility of the closure extending to 48 hours.

309 Response Priorities
The following priorities are general guidelines for response to a pollution incident within the Prince William Sound area. They are based on the premise that the SAFETY OF LIFE IS OF PARAMOUNT IMPORTANCE IN ANY POLLUTION INCIDENT, with property and the environment, although of significant importance, being secondary. Nothing in this subpart, however, is meant to indicate that higher priority items must be completed before performing a lower priority task. They may be carried out simultaneously or in the most logical

sequence considering each individual pollution incident.

a. *Priority One.* Safety of life. For all incidents which may occur within the COTP PWS area of responsibility, the safety of personnel must be the first priority. No personnel are to be sent into an affected area without first determining the hazards involved and the precautions to be taken.
b. *Priority Two.* Stopping or reducing the discharge. Elimination of the pollution source must be attempted quickly to prevent contamination of wildlife habitats and shoreline.
c. *Priority Three.* Safety of the vessel/facility and intact cargo.
d. *Priority Four.* Containment, exclusion or dispersion. In the event that the location of a spill or the weather conditions do not permit open water containment/recovery, protection of the shoreline areas of greatest ecological sensitivity becomes paramount. It is recognized that it may be necessary to make trade-offs in order to achieve optimum overall protection of the environment. The use of dispersants must be considered in accordance with the established guidelines for Prince William Sound.
e. *Priority Five.* Removal and disposal. It may not be possible to protect the entire shoreline from oil and in fact oil may be purposely allowed to come ashore in some areas as an alternative to damaging other areas.

Beach/shoreline cleanup will normally be undertaken only after higher priority items have been considered and/or acted upon.

Shoreline cleanup will be conducted when such removal can be accomplished with lesser environmental damage than actually allowing the oil to naturally weather and biodegrade. The pros and cons of removal methods such as bulk removal of oil and contaminated debris which may cause excessive erosion, and the possible damaging effects to other species by the chemical or mechanical washing of rocks to remove oil, must be carefully weighed.

310 Disposal Operations

310.1 Responsible Party.
Preparations for disposal of recovered material must begin during the early stages of a response. The responsible party must coordinate their efforts with the Coast Guard, EPA, and State of Alaska to ensure that the requirements of the laws and permits governing the storage and transport of recovered materials are met. Temporary storage locations should be identified at the beginning of a response.

310.2 Federal Cleanup.
In the event of the federal assumption of cleanup activities, the contractor will be required to properly dispose of recovered material. The contractor will be responsible for the security of the storage area and shall only store material after it is properly marked and ready for transport. The contractor will be responsible for moving the debris as soon as possible.

405 Description of Billet Duties and Responsibilities

405.1 On-Scene Coordinator Staff.

a. *On-Scene Coordinator.* The Commanding Officer of MSO Valdez is the predesignated Federal On-Scene Coordinator (OSC). The OSC is responsible for the coordination of all federal pollution control efforts at the scene of a spill or potential spill as required by the National and Regional Contingency Plan.
b. *Assistant On-Scene Coordinator.* The Assistant On-Scene Coordinator is responsible to assist the OSC in the coordination and direction of federal pollution control efforts.
c. *Historian/Recordkeeper.* The Historian/Record keeper is responsible for maintaining the OSC's records of the spill. He/she will prepare and maintain a chronological record of important events and generate the POLREPS. This chronology may be used: (a) to develop POLREPS; (b) to augment the spill investigator's report; and (c) as a basis for the OSC's report required by 40 CFR 300.165 of the NCP. On smaller spills this function may be handled by the Watchstander.
d. *VTC Watch Supervisor.* This person is the Watch Supervisor at MSO Valdez and is primarily responsible for vessel traffic in the vicinity of the discharge and works with the Executive Officer for the day to day operation of the unit. The VTC Watch Supervisor is also responsi-

ble for coordinating any Coast Guard search and rescue activities which occur during the response.

e. *Public Affairs Officer.* The Public Affairs Officer will serve to develop and coordinate press releases as directed by the OSC. He/she shall arrange all press conferences and/or interviews. The PAO will be the liaison with the media and will provide access to the cleanup operation when such activities will not interfere with the ongoing cleanup. Further, he/she is responsible for supplying information on PAO activities to the historian for inclusion in the POLREP.

405.2 Operations Officer Staff.

a. *Operations Officer.* He/she functions as Operations Chief in the ICS. It will be the Operations Manager's responsibility to coordinate the actions of the forces operating under the OSC and to ensure that all directions from the OSC are given to appropriate personnel. The Operations Manager has a dual role dependent on the action taken by the spiller.
  1. If the OSC assumes responsibility for the cleanup operation, the Operations Officer supervises the Coast Guard and contractor forces involved in the cleanup. The Operations Officer works with the Planning Officer and Finance Officer to determine the actions to be taken, order the necessary equipment and personnel, and work closely with the civilian contractor to ensure the spill is cleaned in a thorough and efficient manner. Additionally, he/she may have to utilize and integrate other federal agency personnel or civilian volunteers into his/her work force. The Operations Officer also must be alert to see that all safety standards and procedures are followed.
  2. Where the spiller accepts responsibility for the cleanup, the Operations Officer supervises the monitoring of the cleanup activities and reports to the OSC.

b. *Nearshore Cleanup Director.* The Nearshore Cleanup Director is primarily responsible for preparing the overall strategy of tactical booming and the shoreline portion of the cleanup, using the most appropriate methods available, determining equipment and personnel needs, and establishing priority areas for the cleanup to take place. The Nearshore Cleanup Director works for the Operations Officer.

c. *Tactical Booming Officer.* The Tactical Booming Officer is primarily responsible for preparing the overall strategy of the exclusion booming portion of the response, using the most appropriate methods available, determining equipment and personnel needs, and ensuring that priority areas for protection are identified. The Tactical Booming Officer works for the Nearshore Cleanup Director.

d. *Vessel/Air Operations Director.* The Vessel/Air Operations Director is primarily responsible for preparing the vessel and aircraft operations portion of the response. His plan will reflect agency restriction or use guidelines which have an impact on the operational capability during the response. After the plan is approved, Vessel/Air Operations is responsible for implementing the strategic aspects as opposed to those that pertain to specific target selection. Vessel/Air Operations works directly for the Operations Officer.

e. *Wildlife Director.* The Wildlife Director is primarily responsible for establishing a rehabilitation strategy and coordinating the capture and removal of wildlife injured as a result of the discharge, rehabilitation efforts, and records of wildlife damage as a result of the discharge. The Wildlife Director will assign a liaison to work with the Public Affairs Officer who is knowledgeable in the methods being used. The Wildlife Director works for the Operations Officer.

f. *Open-Water Containment Director.* The Open-Water Containment Director is primarily responsible for preparing the overall strategy of the open-water containment portion of the response, using the most appropriate methods available, determining equipment and personnel needs, and making recommendations to the Operations Officer about the use of dispersants. The Open-Water Containment Director works for the Operations Officer.

g. *Mechanical Response Officer.* The Mechanical Response Officer is responsible for monitoring the effectiveness of mechanical recovery efforts and directing/making recommendations about the use of equipment. He works directly for the Open-Water Containment Director.

h. *Non-Mechanical Response Officer.* The Non-Mechanical Response Officer is responsible for making recommendations about the appropriateness and effectiveness of non-traditional methods such as dispersants, burning, or bioremediation. He maintains a close liaison with the responsible party and the SSC. The Non-Mechanical Response Officer works directly for Open-Water Containment Director.

405.3. Source Mitigation/Salvage Staff.

a. *Source Mitigation/Salvage Officer.* The Source Mitigation/Salvage Officer is primarily responsible for preparing the overall strategy of stopping/minimizing the discharge, using the most appropriate methods available to prevent the continuing discharge from the source and making recommendations to the Cleanup Manager about the conduct of salvage operations. The Source Mitigation/Salvage Officer works for the OSC.

405.4 Planning Officer Staff.

a. *Planning Officer.* The Planning Officer works with the Scientific Support Coordinator to understand the current situation, predict a probable course of events, and prepare alternative strategies and control operations for the response. He/she is the Plans Chief under the Incident Command System and works directly for the OSC.

b. *Command Post personnel.* The command post exists as the center of information flow to and from the On-Scene Coordinator. The various personnel staffing the command post manage this flow of information. Depending on the scope and the size of the spill, extra personnel may be assigned to ensure that information is properly managed. They will generally be assigned to the Planning Officer to help ensure that an appropriate flow of information is maintained.

Appendix C — Tide Charts

Valdez, Alaska
Times and Heights of High and Low Waters

October

Day	Time (h m)	Height (ft)	Height (cm)
1 F	0114	11.9	363
	0706	1.7	52
	1310	12.9	393
	1932	0.2	6
2 Sa	0146	11.8	360
	0735	2.2	67
	1335	13.0	396
	2005	0.2	6
3 Su	0217	11.5	351
	0806	2.8	85
	1400	12.9	393
	2037	0.4	12
4 M	0249	11.0	335
	0835	3.4	104
	1425	12.7	387
	2114	0.8	24
5 Tu	0324	10.3	314
	0907	4.1	125
	1455	12.3	375
	2153	1.3	40
6 W	0407	9.6	293
	0945	4.7	143
	1530	11.8	360
	2241	1.8	55
7 Th	0505	9.0	274
	1033	5.3	162
	1614	11.1	338
	2337	2.2	67
8 F ○	0638	8.7	265
	1134	5.6	171
	1729	10.4	317
9 Sa	0042	2.4	73
	0803	9.0	274
	1256	5.6	171
	1919	10.1	308
10 Su	0158	2.3	70
	0902	9.8	299
	1427	4.8	146
	2044	10.6	323
11 M	0312	1.8	55
	0948	10.9	332
	1544	3.3	101
	2150	11.3	344
12 Tu	0408	1.2	37
	1031	12.0	366
	1639	1.5	46
	2247	12.0	366
13 W	0455	0.7	21
	1111	13.2	402
	1730	-0.2	-6
	2340	12.6	384
14 Th	0540	0.4	12
	1151	14.2	433
	1813	-1.6	-49
15 F ●	0032	13.0	396
	0623	0.4	12
	1232	14.9	454
	1858	-2.5	-76
16 Sa	0121	13.1	399
	0705	0.7	21
	1311	15.2	463
	1944	-2.8	-85
17 Su	0209	12.8	390
	0749	1.3	40
	1351	15.0	457
	2029	-2.5	-76
18 M	0258	12.2	372
	0833	2.1	64
	1434	14.4	439
	2119	-1.7	-52
19 Tu	0351	11.4	347
	0921	3.0	91
	1519	13.5	411
	2209	-0.7	-21
20 W	0450	10.6	323
	1012	3.9	119
	1612	12.2	372
	2303	0.5	15
21 Th ○	0603	10.0	305
	1113	4.7	143
	1721	11.0	335
22 F	0003	1.6	49
	0717	9.9	302
	1225	5.2	158
	1851	10.2	311
23 Sa	0113	2.3	70
	0824	10.1	308
	1353	5.0	152
	2014	9.9	302
24 Su	0227	2.7	82
	0917	10.6	323
	1517	4.3	131
	2120	10.0	305
25 M	0331	2.8	85
	1002	11.1	338
	1617	3.2	98
	2216	10.2	311
26 Tu	0421	2.7	82
	1034	11.7	357
	1658	2.2	67
	2303	10.6	323
27 W	0458	2.6	79
	1108	12.2	372
	1735	1.2	37
	2346	10.9	332
28 Th	0533	2.7	82
	1138	12.6	384
	1807	0.5	15
29 F	0023	11.2	341
	0605	2.8	85
	1207	13.0	396
	1839	0.0	0
30 Sa ○	0058	11.3	344
	0637	3.0	91
	1234	13.2	402
	1910	-0.3	-9
31 Su	0132	11.3	344
	0705	3.3	101
	1301	13.3	405
	1942	-0.4	-12

November

Day	Time (h m)	Height (ft)	Height (cm)
1 M	0206	11.2	341
	0737	3.6	110
	1331	13.3	405
	2017	-0.3	-9
2 Tu	0242	10.9	332
	0813	4.0	122
	1401	13.1	399
	2055	0.0	0
3 W	0319	10.5	320
	0846	4.4	134
	1433	12.7	387
	2135	0.4	12
4 Th	0401	10.1	308
	0932	4.8	146
	1510	12.1	369
	2220	0.8	24
5 F	0500	9.8	299
	1022	5.1	155
	1557	11.3	344
	2310	1.3	40
6 Sa ○	0608	9.7	296
	1126	5.2	158
	1707	10.5	320
7 Su	0006	1.7	52
	0718	10.1	308
	1238	4.9	149
	1850	9.9	302
8 M	0110	2.1	64
	0816	10.8	329
	1402	4.0	122
	2019	10.0	305
9 Tu	0218	2.2	67
	0905	11.7	357
	1520	2.5	76
	2128	10.4	317
10 W	0323	2.2	67
	0950	12.7	387
	1623	0.8	24
	2232	11.0	335
11 Th	0423	2.0	61
	1034	13.7	418
	1713	-0.9	-27
	2332	11.5	351
12 F	0511	1.9	58
	1119	14.5	442
	1801	-2.1	-64
13 Sa ●	0025	11.9	363
	0600	1.8	55
	1204	15.0	457
	1845	-2.9	-88
14 Su	0115	12.2	372
	0645	2.0	61
	1248	15.1	460
	1929	-3.0	-91
15 M	0204	12.2	372
	0731	2.3	70
	1331	14.8	451
	2015	-2.7	-82
16 Tu	0252	11.9	363
	0816	2.7	82
	1417	14.2	433
	2100	-2.0	-61
17 W	0340	11.5	351
	0905	3.3	101
	1502	13.2	402
	2148	-1.0	-30
18 Th	0433	11.0	335
	0957	3.9	119
	1550	12.1	369
	2236	0.1	3
19 F	0529	10.6	323
	1054	4.4	134
	1649	10.8	329
	2326	1.2	37
20 Sa ○	0632	10.5	320
	1157	4.7	143
	1804	9.8	299
21 Su	0018	2.2	67
	0732	10.5	320
	1309	4.6	140
	1927	9.2	280
22 M	0118	3.0	91
	0824	10.8	329
	1432	4.1	125
	2039	9.0	274
23 Tu	0221	3.6	110
	0905	11.2	341
	1542	3.2	98
	2141	9.1	277
24 W	0323	3.9	119
	0944	11.6	354
	1631	2.2	67
	2234	9.4	287
25 Th	0413	4.0	122
	1021	12.0	366
	1709	1.3	40
	2324	9.8	299
26 F	0457	4.0	122
	1056	12.4	378
	1746	0.4	12
27 Sa	0009	10.2	311
	0533	3.9	119
	1132	12.8	390
	1820	-0.2	-6
28 Su ○	0046	10.5	320
	0609	3.9	119
	1204	13.1	399
	1852	-0.7	-21
29 M	0124	10.7	326
	0644	3.8	116
	1238	13.3	405
	1927	-1.0	-30
30 Tu	0159	10.9	332
	0719	3.8	116
	1310	13.4	408
	2002	-1.1	-34

December

Day	Time (h m)	Height (ft)	Height (cm)
1 W	0235	10.9	332
	0757	3.9	119
	1346	13.2	402
	2039	-1.0	-30
2 Th	0313	10.8	329
	0839	4.0	122
	1424	12.9	393
	2119	-0.8	-24
3 F	0352	10.8	329
	0922	4.1	125
	1503	12.3	375
	2201	-0.3	-9
4 Sa	0438	10.7	326
	1015	4.1	125
	1551	11.5	351
	2246	0.3	9
5 Su	0529	10.8	329
	1115	3.9	119
	1654	10.4	317
	2334	1.0	30
6 M ○	0629	11.0	335
	1221	3.6	110
	1821	9.6	293
7 Tu	0029	1.8	55
	0727	11.5	351
	1335	2.9	88
	1953	9.2	280
8 W	0131	2.6	79
	0822	12.1	369
	1453	1.7	52
	2112	9.3	283
9 Th	0241	3.1	94
	0915	12.8	390
	1602	0.3	9
	2223	9.7	296
10 F	0350	3.2	98
	1005	13.5	411
	1701	-1.0	-30
	2326	10.3	314
11 Sa	0450	3.0	91
	1056	14.0	427
	1748	-2.1	-64
12 Su	0022	10.8	329
	0543	2.8	85
	1146	14.3	436
	1834	-2.7	-82
13 M ●	0111	11.3	344
	0631	2.6	79
	1233	14.4	439
	1919	-2.9	-88
14 Tu	0158	11.6	354
	0719	2.5	76
	1320	14.2	433
	2002	-2.7	-82
15 W	0242	11.7	357
	0805	2.6	79
	1406	13.7	418
	2044	-2.2	-67
16 Th	0324	11.6	354
	0850	2.8	85
	1448	12.9	393
	2124	-1.3	-40
17 F	0406	11.4	347
	0937	3.1	94
	1530	11.9	363
	2207	-0.3	-9
18 Sa	0448	11.1	338
	1028	3.5	107
	1615	10.8	329
	2248	0.8	24
19 Su	0534	10.9	332
	1121	3.8	116
	1711	9.6	293
	2328	1.9	58
20 M ○	0622	10.7	326
	1216	3.9	119
	1824	8.7	265
21 Tu	0012	3.0	91
	0714	10.7	326
	1326	3.8	116
	1943	8.1	247
22 W	0101	3.9	119
	0803	10.8	329
	1443	3.3	101
	2057	8.0	244
23 Th	0203	4.6	140
	0853	11.1	338
	1554	2.5	76
	2203	8.3	253
24 F	0317	5.0	152
	0936	11.4	347
	1643	1.6	49
	2303	8.7	265
25 Sa	0418	4.9	149
	1018	11.8	360
	1724	0.6	18
	2353	9.2	280
26 Su	0506	4.6	140
	1101	12.3	375
	1801	-0.2	-6
27 M	0033	9.8	299
	0546	4.2	128
	1143	12.7	387
	1836	-1.0	-30
28 Tu	0112	10.3	314
	0625	3.8	116
	1223	13.1	399
	1910	-1.5	-46
29 W	0147	10.8	329
	0704	3.4	104
	1302	13.3	405
	1946	-1.9	-58
30 Th	0221	11.2	341
	0745	3.0	91
	1340	13.4	408
	2022	-1.9	-58
31 F	0255	11.5	351
	0828	2.7	82
	1419	13.1	399
	2100	-1.7	-52

Time meridian 135° W. 0000 is midnight. 1200 is noon.
Heights are referred to mean lower low water which is the chart datum of soundings.

San Diego, California
Times and Heights of High and Low Waters

October

Day	Time (h m)	Height (ft)	Height (cm)	Day	Time (h m)	Height (ft)	Height (cm)
1 F	0248 / 0859 / 1528 / 2133	1.1 / 6.0 / 0.4 / 4.8	34 / 183 / 12 / 146	16 Sa	0251 / 0904 / 1553 / 2210	0.9 / 7.4 / -1.3 / 5.0	27 / 226 / -40 / 152
2 Sa	0310 / 0924 / 1600 / 2206	1.4 / 6.0 / 0.4 / 4.5	43 / 183 / 12 / 137	17 Su	0328 / 0944 / 1645 / 2307	1.3 / 7.3 / -1.1 / 4.6	40 / 223 / -34 / 140
3 Su	0332 / 0946 / 1636 / 2244	1.7 / 5.9 / 0.5 / 4.1	52 / 180 / 15 / 125	18 M	0410 / 1029 / 1741	1.8 / 6.9 / -0.7	55 / 210 / -21
4 M	0353 / 1014 / 1718 / 2330	2.0 / 5.8 / 0.7 / 3.7	61 / 177 / 21 / 113	19 Tu	0013 / 0457 / 1118 / 1844	4.1 / 2.3 / 6.3 / -0.2	125 / 70 / 192 / -6
5 Tu	0412 / 1043 / 1808	2.4 / 5.6 / 0.9	73 / 171 / 27	20 W	0133 / 0557 / 1215 / 1956	3.9 / 2.8 / 5.7 / 0.2	119 / 85 / 174 / 6
6 W	0034 / 0440 / 1126 / 1919	3.3 / 2.7 / 5.4 / 1.0	101 / 82 / 165 / 30	21 Th	0309 / 0731 / 1333 / 2112	3.9 / 3.1 / 5.1 / 0.4	119 / 94 / 155 / 12
7 Th	0222 / 0515 / 1229 / 2044	3.2 / 3.0 / 5.1 / 1.0	98 / 91 / 155 / 30	22 F ☽	0429 / 0930 / 1445 / 2220	4.2 / 3.0 / 4.8 / 0.5	128 / 91 / 146 / 15
8 F ○	0421 / 0730 / 1403 / 2200	3.5 / 3.3 / 4.9 / 0.8	107 / 101 / 149 / 24	23 Sa	0521 / 1055 / 1628 / 2313	4.6 / 2.5 / 4.7 / 0.6	140 / 76 / 143 / 18
9 Sa	0511 / 0946 / 1541 / 2256	4.0 / 3.0 / 5.0 / 0.5	122 / 91 / 152 / 15	24 Su	0556 / 1151 / 1732 / 2354	5.0 / 2.0 / 4.7 / 0.7	152 / 61 / 143 / 21
10 Su	0541 / 1105 / 1653 / 2340	4.5 / 2.4 / 5.3 / 0.2	137 / 73 / 162 / 6	25 M	0625 / 1236 / 1823	5.3 / 1.4 / 4.7	162 / 43 / 143
11 M	0614 / 1159 / 1756	5.1 / 1.5 / 5.6	155 / 46 / 171	26 Tu	0028 / 0652 / 1309 / 1908	0.8 / 5.6 / 0.9 / 4.7	24 / 171 / 27 / 143
12 Tu	0021 / 0643 / 1247 / 1851	0.1 / 5.8 / 0.6 / 5.8	3 / 177 / 18 / 177	27 W	0057 / 0715 / 1344 / 1944	1.0 / 5.9 / 0.5 / 4.7	30 / 180 / 15 / 143
13 W	0100 / 0715 / 1334 / 1940	0.1 / 6.4 / -0.2 / 5.9	3 / 195 / -6 / 180	28 Th	0122 / 0738 / 1415 / 2019	1.2 / 6.1 / 0.2 / 4.6	37 / 186 / 6 / 140
14 Th	0136 / 0750 / 1419 / 2029	0.2 / 6.9 / -0.8 / 5.8	6 / 210 / -24 / 177	29 F	0147 / 0801 / 1445 / 2054	1.4 / 6.2 / -0.1 / 4.5	43 / 189 / -3 / 137
15 F ●	0214 / 0826 / 1505 / 2119	0.5 / 7.3 / -1.2 / 5.5	15 / 223 / -37 / 168	30 Sa ◐	0212 / 0824 / 1516 / 2130	1.6 / 6.3 / -0.2 / 4.3	49 / 192 / -6 / 131
				31 Su	0237 / 0850 / 1548 / 2206	1.8 / 6.3 / -0.2 / 4.1	55 / 192 / -6 / 125

November

Day	Time (h m)	Height (ft)	Height (cm)	Day	Time (h m)	Height (ft)	Height (cm)
1 M	0259 / 0918 / 1627 / 2246	2.0 / 6.3 / -0.1 / 3.9	61 / 192 / -3 / 119	16 Tu	0351 / 1008 / 1724	2.0 / 6.9 / -1.1	61 / 210 / -34
2 Tu	0324 / 0947 / 1706 / 2334	2.3 / 6.1 / 0.0 / 3.7	70 / 186 / 0 / 113	17 W	0002 / 0440 / 1052 / 1815	4.2 / 2.4 / 6.3 / -0.6	128 / 73 / 192 / -18
3 W	0356 / 1022 / 1751	2.5 / 5.9 / 0.2	76 / 180 / 6	18 Th	0104 / 0539 / 1144 / 1913	4.1 / 2.7 / 5.6 / -0.1	125 / 82 / 171 / -3
4 Th	0034 / 0435 / 1104 / 1848	3.5 / 2.8 / 5.6 / 0.4	107 / 85 / 171 / 12	19 F	0220 / 0701 / 1247 / 2010	4.1 / 3.0 / 4.9 / 0.4	125 / 91 / 149 / 12
5 F	0153 / 0539 / 1203 / 1951	3.6 / 3.1 / 5.2 / 0.5	110 / 94 / 158 / 15	20 Sa ☽	0325 / 0845 / 1403 / 2110	4.3 / 2.9 / 4.3 / 0.8	131 / 88 / 131 / 24
6 Sa ○	0312 / 0731 / 1322 / 2058	3.8 / 3.1 / 4.8 / 0.6	116 / 94 / 146 / 18	21 Su	0421 / 1023 / 1536 / 2206	4.6 / 2.5 / 3.9 / 1.0	140 / 76 / 119 / 30
7 Su	0408 / 0930 / 1505 / 2158	4.3 / 2.7 / 4.6 / 0.6	131 / 82 / 140 / 18	22 M	0503 / 1129 / 1658 / 2255	5.0 / 1.9 / 3.8 / 1.3	152 / 58 / 116 / 40
8 M	0450 / 1047 / 1631 / 2252	4.9 / 1.9 / 4.6 / 0.6	149 / 58 / 140 / 18	23 Tu	0537 / 1215 / 1801 / 2336	5.3 / 1.3 / 3.8 / 1.5	162 / 40 / 116 / 46
9 Tu	0529 / 1150 / 1740 / 2337	5.6 / 1.0 / 4.7 / 0.7	171 / 30 / 143 / 21	24 W	0606 / 1257 / 1851	5.6 / 0.7 / 3.9	171 / 21 / 119
10 W	0606 / 1240 / 1843	6.3 / 0.1 / 4.9	192 / 3 / 149	25 Th	0011 / 0638 / 1329 / 1937	1.6 / 5.9 / 0.3 / 4.0	49 / 180 / 9 / 122
11 Th	0022 / 0643 / 1329 / 1939	0.8 / 6.9 / -0.8 / 5.0	24 / 210 / -24 / 152	26 F	0043 / 0703 / 1404 / 2015	1.7 / 6.1 / -0.1 / 4.0	52 / 186 / -3 / 122
12 F	0103 / 0722 / 1414 / 2029	0.9 / 7.3 / -1.3 / 4.9	27 / 223 / -40 / 149	27 Sa	0115 / 0731 / 1436 / 2051	1.8 / 6.4 / -0.4 / 4.1	55 / 195 / -12 / 125
13 Sa ●	0145 / 0802 / 1459 / 2121	1.1 / 7.6 / -1.6 / 4.8	34 / 232 / -49 / 146	28 Su	0143 / 0800 / 1508 / 2127	1.9 / 6.5 / -0.6 / 4.0	58 / 198 / -18 / 122
14 Su	0227 / 0841 / 1548 / 2211	1.4 / 7.6 / -1.7 / 4.6	43 / 232 / -52 / 140	29 M	0212 / 0831 / 1540 / 2204	2.0 / 6.6 / -0.7 / 4.0	61 / 201 / -21 / 122
15 M	0309 / 0923 / 1633 / 2303	1.7 / 7.4 / -1.5 / 4.4	52 / 226 / -46 / 134	30 Tu	0244 / 0900 / 1616 / 2241	2.1 / 6.5 / -0.7 / 3.9	64 / 198 / -21 / 119

December

Day	Time (h m)	Height (ft)	Height (cm)	Day	Time (h m)	Height (ft)	Height (cm)
1 W	0316 / 0935 / 1653 / 2326	2.3 / 6.4 / -0.6 / 3.9	70 / 195 / -18 / 119	16 Th	0430 / 1033 / 1742	2.1 / 6.2 / -0.7	64 / 189 / -21
2 Th	0356 / 1011 / 1734	2.4 / 6.2 / -0.4	73 / 189 / -12	17 F	0021 / 0518 / 1112 / 1821	4.4 / 2.4 / 5.5 / -0.1	134 / 73 / 168 / -3
3 F	0015 / 0447 / 1056 / 1817	3.9 / 2.6 / 5.8 / -0.2	119 / 79 / 177 / -6	18 Sa	0112 / 0621 / 1200 / 1904	4.3 / 2.6 / 4.8 / 0.4	131 / 79 / 146 / 12
4 Sa	0109 / 0552 / 1149 / 1906	4.1 / 2.7 / 5.2 / 0.1	125 / 82 / 158 / 3	19 Su	0203 / 0740 / 1257 / 1949	4.4 / 2.6 / 4.1 / 1.0	134 / 79 / 125 / 30
5 Su	0206 / 0721 / 1300 / 2002	4.3 / 2.6 / 4.6 / 0.5	131 / 79 / 140 / 15	20 M ☽	0258 / 0921 / 1419 / 2039	4.5 / 2.4 / 3.4 / 1.4	137 / 73 / 104 / 43
6 M ○	0305 / 0904 / 1433 / 2102	4.8 / 2.2 / 4.1 / 0.8	146 / 67 / 125 / 24	21 Tu	0354 / 1050 / 1609 / 2134	4.8 / 2.0 / 3.1 / 1.8	146 / 61 / 94 / 55
7 Tu	0357 / 1033 / 1612 / 2202	5.3 / 1.5 / 3.9 / 1.1	162 / 46 / 119 / 34	22 W	0439 / 1156 / 1741 / 2229	5.0 / 1.4 / 3.1 / 2.0	152 / 43 / 94 / 61
8 W	0447 / 1141 / 1737 / 2300	5.9 / 0.6 / 3.9 / 1.3	180 / 18 / 119 / 40	23 Th	0521 / 1241 / 1847 / 2322	5.4 / 0.8 / 3.3 / 2.2	165 / 24 / 101 / 67
9 Th	0533 / 1237 / 1843 / 2352	6.5 / -0.3 / 4.1 / 1.5	198 / -9 / 125 / 46	24 F	0559 / 1316 / 1934	5.7 / 0.2 / 3.5	174 / 6 / 107
10 F	0619 / 1327 / 1942	7.0 / -1.0 / 4.3	213 / -30 / 131	25 Sa	0007 / 0635 / 1351 / 2013	2.2 / 6.0 / -0.2 / 3.7	67 / 183 / -6 / 113
11 Sa	0041 / 0705 / 1412 / 2034	1.5 / 7.3 / -1.5 / 4.4	46 / 223 / -46 / 134	26 Su	0046 / 0708 / 1424 / 2046	2.2 / 6.3 / -0.6 / 3.9	67 / 192 / -18 / 119
12 Su	0130 / 0747 / 1456 / 2120	1.6 / 7.5 / -1.8 / 4.5	49 / 229 / -55 / 137	27 M	0124 / 0743 / 1456 / 2118	2.1 / 6.6 / -0.9 / 4.0	64 / 201 / -27 / 122
13 M ●	0212 / 0829 / 1539 / 2204	1.7 / 7.5 / -1.8 / 4.5	52 / 229 / -55 / 137	28 Tu	0200 / 0815 / 1527 / 2150	2.0 / 6.7 / -1.1 / 4.2	61 / 204 / -34 / 128
14 Tu	0258 / 0911 / 1621 / 2251	1.8 / 7.2 / -1.5 / 4.5	55 / 219 / -46 / 137	29 W	0238 / 0851 / 1559 / 2225	1.9 / 6.8 / -1.1 / 4.3	58 / 207 / -34 / 131
15 W	0344 / 0952 / 1702 / 2336	1.9 / 6.8 / -1.2 / 4.4	58 / 207 / -37 / 134	30 Th	0318 / 0929 / 1633 / 2259	1.9 / 6.7 / -1.0 / 4.4	58 / 204 / -30 / 134
				31 F	0401 / 1008 / 1707 / 2339	1.9 / 6.3 / -0.8 / 4.6	58 / 192 / -24 / 140

Time meridian 120° W. 0000 is midnight. 1200 is noon.
Heights are referred to mean lower low water which is the chart datum of soundings.

Oil Spill!

Galveston, Texas
Times and Heights of High and Low Waters

October						November						December					
Time	Height		Time	Height		Time	Height		Time	Height		Time	Height		Time	Height	
	h m	ft	cm	h m	ft	cm	h m	ft	cm	h m	ft	cm	h m	ft	cm	h m	ft	cm

October

1 F: 0341 1.5 46; 1013 0.6 18; 1705 1.6 49; 2244 1.1 34
2 Sa: 0350 1.5 46; 1041 0.5 15; 1750 1.6 49; 2317 1.2 37
3 Su: 0359 1.5 46; 1109 0.5 15; 1843 1.6 49; 2345 1.3 40
4 M: 0408 1.5 46; 1145 0.4 12; 1942 1.6 49
5 Tu: 0024 1.4 43; 0415 1.5 46; 1224 0.4 12; 2111 1.6 49
6 W: 0109 1.5 46; 0419 1.6 49; 1319 0.3 9; 2248 1.6 49
7 Th: 0250 1.5 46; 0400 1.6 49; 1420 0.3 9
8 F ☉: 0002 1.7 52; 1532 0.3 9
9 Sa: 0041 1.7 52; 1644 0.4 12
10 Su: 0106 1.7 52; 0649 1.3 40; 1007 1.4 43; 1753 0.4 12
11 M: 0126 1.7 52; 0711 1.2 37; 1202 1.5 46; 1856 0.5 15
12 Tu: 0149 1.7 52; 0743 0.9 27; 1330 1.6 49; 1951 0.6 18
13 W: 0208 1.6 49; 0815 0.6 18; 1440 1.8 55; 2047 0.8 24
14 Th: 0228 1.6 49; 0854 0.4 12; 1550 1.9 58; 2139 1.0 30
15 F ●: 0248 1.6 49; 0936 0.2 6; 1652 1.9 58; 2231 1.2 37
16 Sa: 0312 1.6 49; 1021 0.0 0; 1757 2.0 61; 2324 1.3 40
17 Su: 0337 1.6 49; 1105 -0.1 -3; 1904 1.9 58
18 M: 0016 1.5 46; 0359 1.7 52; 1157 -0.1 -3; 2015 1.9 58
19 Tu: 0114 1.6 49; 0424 1.7 52; 1251 0.0 0; 2139 1.8 55
20 W: 0234 1.5 46; 0439 1.6 49; 1352 0.1 3; 2251 1.8 55
21 Th: 1458 0.3 9; 2354 1.7 52
22 F ☉: 1609 0.4 12
23 Sa: 0035 1.6 49; 0638 1.2 37; 0929 1.3 40; 1719 0.5 15
24 Su: 0102 1.6 49; 0703 1.1 34; 1135 1.3 40; 1822 0.7 21
25 M: 0122 1.5 46; 0725 1.0 30; 1303 1.4 43; 1916 0.8 24
26 Tu: 0137 1.5 46; 0753 0.8 24; 1409 1.5 46; 2008 0.9 27
27 W: 0153 1.4 43; 0820 0.6 18; 1501 1.5 46; 2047 1.0 30
28 Th: 0205 1.4 43; 0847 0.5 15; 1550 1.6 49; 2127 1.1 34
29 F: 0217 1.4 43; 0912 0.4 12; 1632 1.6 49; 2205 1.2 37
30 Sa ○: 0228 1.4 43; 0939 0.3 9; 1717 1.7 52; 2241 1.2 37
31 Su: 0243 1.4 43; 1009 0.2 6; 1803 1.7 52; 2316 1.3 40

November

1 M: 0251 1.4 43; 1042 0.2 6; 1851 1.7 52; 2353 1.4 43
2 Tu: 0302 1.5 46; 1120 0.1 3; 1947 1.7 52
3 W: 0041 1.4 43; 0318 1.5 46; 1205 0.1 3; 2046 1.6 49
4 Th: 1251 0.1 3; 2149 1.6 49
5 F: 1348 0.2 6; 2239 1.6 49
6 Sa: 1454 0.3 9; 2314 1.6 49
7 Su ○: 0518 1.1 34; 0818 1.2 37; 1605 0.4 12; 2340 1.5 46
8 M: 0553 0.9 27; 1049 1.2 37; 1718 0.6 18
9 Tu: 0005 1.5 46; 0629 0.7 21; 1236 1.4 43; 1830 0.7 21
10 W: 0030 1.4 43; 0707 0.4 12; 1357 1.5 46; 1939 0.9 27
11 Th: 0054 1.4 43; 0747 0.1 3; 1506 1.7 52; 2042 1.0 30
12 F: 0116 1.4 43; 0830 -0.1 -3; 1612 1.8 55; 2142 1.2 37
13 Sa ●: 0148 1.5 46; 0916 -0.3 -9; 1710 1.9 58; 2235 1.3 40
14 Su: 0213 1.5 46; 1002 -0.4 -12; 1806 1.8 55; 2327 1.4 43
15 M: 0245 1.5 46; 1048 -0.4 -12; 1905 1.8 55
16 Tu: 0015 1.4 43; 0314 1.5 46; 1137 -0.3 -9; 2001 1.7 52
17 W: 0109 1.3 40; 0352 1.4 43; 1230 -0.2 -6; 2058 1.6 49
18 Th: 0208 1.3 40; 0439 1.4 43; 1320 0.0 0; 2151 1.5 46
19 F: 0330 1.1 34; 0537 1.2 37; 1417 0.2 6; 2233 1.4 43
20 Sa ☽: 0433 1.0 30; 0723 1.1 34; 1517 0.4 12; 2305 1.3 40
21 Su: 0525 0.9 27; 0943 1.0 30; 1623 0.5 15; 2328 1.3 40
22 M: 0602 0.7 21; 1148 1.0 30; 1731 0.7 21; 2347 1.2 37
23 Tu: 0639 0.5 15; 1318 1.1 34; 1837 0.8 24
24 W: 0007 1.2 37; 0710 0.3 9; 1424 1.2 37; 1940 0.9 27
25 Th: 0027 1.2 37; 0742 0.2 6; 1513 1.3 40; 2033 1.0 30
26 F: 0045 1.2 37; 0814 0.1 3; 1558 1.4 43; 2123 1.0 30
27 Sa: 0101 1.2 37; 0842 0.0 0; 1640 1.4 43; 2206 1.1 34
28 Su: 0122 1.2 37; 0917 -0.1 -3; 1722 1.5 46; 2244 1.1 34
29 M ○: 0144 1.2 37; 0950 -0.2 -6; 1804 1.5 46; 2320 1.1 34
30 Tu: 0206 1.2 37; 1027 -0.3 -9; 1850 1.5 46; 2354 1.1 34

December

1 W: 0231 1.2 37; 1107 -0.3 -9; 1932 1.4 43
2 Th: 0036 1.1 34; 0309 1.2 37; 1148 -0.3 -9; 2013 1.4 43
3 F: 0125 1.1 34; 0408 1.2 37; 1236 -0.2 -6; 2047 1.4 43
4 Sa: 0221 1.0 30; 0521 1.1 34; 1325 0.0 0; 2119 1.3 40
5 Su: 0319 0.8 24; 0707 1.0 30; 1421 0.2 6; 2148 1.2 37
6 M ☽: 0412 0.6 18; 0921 0.9 27; 1530 0.4 12; 2214 1.2 37
7 Tu: 0504 0.3 9; 1130 1.0 30; 1647 0.6 18; 2241 1.1 34
8 W: 0551 0.0 0; 1313 1.1 34; 1815 0.8 24; 2306 1.1 34
9 Th: 0641 -0.2 -6; 1429 1.3 40; 1937 0.9 27; 2341 1.1 34
10 F: 0727 -0.5 -15; 1531 1.5 46; 2047 1.0 30
11 Sa: 0013 1.2 37; 0815 -0.6 -18; 1627 1.5 46; 2146 1.1 34
12 Su: 0049 1.2 37; 0902 -0.7 -21; 1719 1.5 46; 2235 1.1 34
13 M ●: 0131 1.2 37; 0950 -0.7 -21; 1806 1.5 46; 2318 1.1 34
14 Tu: 0221 1.2 37; 1037 -0.7 -21; 1851 1.4 43; 2354 1.1 34
15 W: 0309 1.2 37; 1122 -0.6 -18; 1931 1.3 40
16 Th: 0035 1.0 30; 0400 1.1 34; 1207 -0.4 -12; 2009 1.2 37
17 F: 0122 0.9 27; 0459 1.0 30; 1246 -0.2 -6; 2039 1.1 34
18 Sa: 0214 0.7 21; 0609 0.9 27; 1332 0.0 0; 2103 1.0 30
19 Su: 0309 0.6 18; 0738 0.7 21; 1421 0.2 6; 2127 1.0 30
20 M: 0407 0.4 12; 0935 0.7 21; 1507 0.4 12; 2146 0.9 27
21 Tu: 0500 0.2 6; 1147 0.7 21; 1618 0.6 18; 2207 0.9 27
22 W: 0545 0.1 3; 1323 0.8 24; 1749 0.7 21; 2229 0.9 27
23 Th: 0625 -0.1 -3; 1429 0.9 27; 1917 0.8 24; 2254 0.9 27
24 F: 0703 -0.2 -6; 1520 1.0 30; 2030 0.8 24; 2329 0.9 27
25 Sa: 0742 -0.3 -9; 1559 1.1 34; 2123 0.8 24; 2354 0.9 27
26 Su: 0820 -0.4 -12; 1640 1.2 37; 2159 0.8 24
27 M: 0033 0.9 27; 0857 -0.5 -15; 1716 1.2 37; 2228 0.8 24
28 Tu ○: 0113 0.9 27; 0937 -0.6 -18; 1751 1.2 37; 2257 0.9 27
29 W: 0157 1.0 30; 1014 -0.6 -18; 1822 1.2 37; 2325 0.8 24
30 Th: 0250 1.0 30; 1056 -0.6 -18; 1852 1.2 37
31 F: 0003 0.8 24; 0348 0.9 27; 1135 -0.5 -15; 1920 1.1 34

Time meridian 90° W. 0000 is midnight. 1200 is noon.
Heights are referred to mean lower low water which is the chart datum of soundings.
On days when the tide is diurnal, high water has an approximate stand of about 7 hours. Predictions are for beginning of stand.

Appendix C

Pensacola, Florida
Times and Heights of High and Low Waters

October

Day	Time (h m)	Height (ft)	Height (cm)	Day	Time (h m)	Height (ft)	Height (cm)
1 F	0738 / 2240	0.6 / 1.4	18 / 43	16 Sa	0849 / 2257	0.1 / 1.9	3 / 58
2 Sa	0839 / 2312	0.5 / 1.5	15 / 46	17 Su	0958 / 2346	0.0 / 1.9	0 / 58
3 Su	0938 / 2352	0.4 / 1.6	12 / 49	18 M	1103	−0.1	−3
4 M	1037	0.4	12	19 Tu	0039 / 1206	1.9 / −0.1	58 / −3
5 Tu	0031 / 1138	1.6 / 0.3	49 / 9	20 W	0133 / 1308	1.9 / 0.0	58 / 0
6 W	0118 / 1238	1.7 / 0.3	52 / 9	21 Th	0228 / 1400	1.7 / 0.1	52 / 3
7 Th	0210 / 1334	1.7 / 0.2	52 / 6	22 F	0321 / 1450	1.6 / 0.3	49 / 9 ◐
8 F	0303 / 1431	1.7 / 0.2	52 / 6 ●	23 Sa	0412 / 1519	1.4 / 0.4	43 / 12
9 Sa	0402 / 1522	1.6 / 0.3	49 / 9	24 Su	0518 / 1527	1.2 / 0.6	37 / 18
10 Su	0511 / 1559	1.5 / 0.4	46 / 12	25 M	0654 / 1503 / 2147	1.0 / 0.7 / 0.9	30 / 21 / 27
11 M	0641 / 1624	1.4 / 0.6	43 / 18	26 Tu	0426 / 1009 / 1312 / 2057	0.7 / 0.8 / 0.7 / 1.0	21 / 24 / 21 / 30
12 Tu	0830 / 1611 / 2151	1.2 / 0.8 / 1.0	37 / 24 / 30	27 W	0551 / 2057	0.6 / 1.2	18 / 37
13 W	0433 / 1150 / 1403 / 2124	0.8 / 1.0 / 0.9 / 1.2	24 / 30 / 27 / 37	28 Th	0651 / 2116	0.5 / 1.3	15 / 40
14 Th	0624 / 2137	0.5 / 1.5	15 / 46	29 F	0730 / 2141	0.3 / 1.4	9 / 43
15 F	0743 / 2213	0.3 / 1.7	9 / 52 ●	30 Sa	0812 / 2213	0.2 / 1.5	6 / 46 ○
				31 Su	0857 / 2248	0.1 / 1.6	3 / 49

November

Day	Time (h m)	Height (ft)	Height (cm)	Day	Time (h m)	Height (ft)	Height (cm)
1 M	0939 / 2324	0.1 / 1.6	3 / 49	16 Tu	1051	−0.4	−12
2 Tu	1025	0.0	0	17 W	0019 / 1140	1.7 / −0.3	52 / −9
3 W	0003 / 1111	1.6 / 0.0	49 / 0	18 Th	0107 / 1230	1.6 / −0.1	49 / −3
4 Th	0046 / 1200	1.6 / 0.0	49 / 0	19 F	0149 / 1305	1.4 / 0.0	43 / 0
5 F	0132 / 1249	1.6 / 0.0	49 / 0	20 Sa	0227 / 1324	1.2 / 0.2	37 / 6 ◐
6 Sa	0218 / 1325	1.5 / 0.1	46 / 3	21 Su	0242 / 1313	1.0 / 0.4	30 / 12
7 Su	0304 / 1354	1.3 / 0.3	40 / 9	22 M	0030 / 1212 / 2045	0.8 / 0.5 / 0.8	24 / 15 / 24
8 M	0350 / 1351 / 2222	1.1 / 0.5 / 0.8	34 / 15 / 24	23 Tu	0826 / 2000	0.5 / 0.9	15 / 27
9 Tu	1254 / 2030	0.6 / 1.0	18 / 30	24 W	0622 / 2001	0.3 / 1.1	9 / 34
10 W	0532 / 2021	0.5 / 1.2	15 / 37	25 Th	0637 / 2023	0.1 / 1.2	3 / 37
11 Th	0624 / 2039	0.2 / 1.5	6 / 46	26 F	0709 / 2048	0.0 / 1.3	0 / 40
12 F	0716 / 2118	−0.1 / 1.7	−3 / 52	27 Sa	0741 / 2123	−0.1 / 1.4	−3 / 43
13 Sa	0811 / 2157	−0.3 / 1.8	−9 / 55 ●	28 Su	0816 / 2155	−0.2 / 1.4	−6 / 43
14 Su	0900 / 2243	−0.4 / 1.9	−12 / 58	29 M	0852 / 2231	−0.3 / 1.5	−9 / 46 ○
15 M	0956 / 2332	−0.4 / 1.8	−12 / 55	30 Tu	0932 / 2311	−0.3 / 1.5	−9 / 46

December

Day	Time (h m)	Height (ft)	Height (cm)	Day	Time (h m)	Height (ft)	Height (cm)
1 W	1014 / 2350	−0.3 / 1.5	−9 / 46	16 Th	0006 / 1112	1.4 / −0.4	43 / −12
2 Th	1053	−0.3	−9	17 F	0041 / 1144	1.2 / −0.2	37 / −6
3 F	0026 / 1129	1.4 / −0.3	43 / −9	18 Sa	0106 / 1145	1.0 / 0.0	30 / 0
4 Sa	0106 / 1154	1.3 / −0.1	40 / −3	19 Su	0121 / 1132 / 2348	0.7 / 0.1 / 0.5	21 / 3 / 15
5 Su	0131 / 1209	1.1 / 0.0	34 / 0	20 M	1028 / 1927	0.2 / 0.6	6 / 18 ◐
6 M	0136 / 1145 / 2029	0.8 / 0.2 / 0.7	24 / 6 / 21	21 Tu	0808 / 1854	0.2 / 0.7	6 / 21
7 Tu	0958 / 1915	0.3 / 0.8	9 / 24	22 W	0618 / 1855	0.0 / 0.8	0 / 24
8 W	0542 / 1914	0.1 / 1.1	3 / 34	23 Th	0612 / 1919	−0.1 / 1.0	−3 / 30
9 Th	0600 / 1939	−0.2 / 1.3	−6 / 40	24 F	0629 / 1951	−0.3 / 1.1	−9 / 34
10 F	0639 / 2018	−0.4 / 1.5	−12 / 46	25 Sa	0701 / 2024	−0.4 / 1.2	−12 / 37
11 Sa	0721 / 2101	−0.6 / 1.6	−18 / 49	26 Su	0734 / 2103	−0.5 / 1.2	−15 / 37
12 Su	0813 / 2147	−0.7 / 1.6	−21 / 49	27 M	0811 / 2141	−0.5 / 1.3	−15 / 40
13 M	0901 / 2238	−0.7 / 1.6	−21 / 49 ●	28 Tu	0846 / 2223	−0.6 / 1.3	−18 / 40 ○
14 Tu	0951 / 2324	−0.6 / 1.5	−18 / 46	29 W	0922 / 2258	−0.6 / 1.3	−18 / 40
15 W	1037	−0.5	−15	30 Th	0957 / 2340	−0.5 / 1.2	−15 / 37
				31 F	1027	−0.4	−12

Time meridian 90° W. 0000 is midnight. 1200 is noon.
Heights are referred to mean lower low water which is the chart datum of soundings.

62 *Oil Spill!*

Charleston, South Carolina
Times and Heights of High and Low Waters

October

	Time	Height ft	Height cm		Time	Height ft	Height cm
1 F	0143 0755 1407 2014	0.5 6.1 0.7 5.6	15 186 21 171	16 Sa	0148 0813 1426 2029	-0.5 7.3 -0.3 6.3	-15 223 -9 192
2 Sa	0219 0830 1445 2046	0.5 6.1 0.8 5.5	15 186 24 168	17 Su	0236 0906 1517 2121	-0.5 7.3 -0.1 6.1	-15 223 -3 186
3 Su	0254 0902 1522 2117	0.6 6.0 0.9 5.3	18 183 27 162	18 M	0326 0959 1609 2213	-0.2 7.1 0.2 5.8	-6 216 6 177
4 M	0328 0936 1559 2149	0.7 6.0 1.1 5.1	21 183 34 155	19 Tu	0417 1053 1702 2308	0.1 6.7 0.5 5.5	3 204 15 168
5 Tu	0405 1013 1640 2223	0.8 5.9 1.3 5.0	24 180 40 152	20 W	0509 1150 1758	0.4 6.4 0.8	12 195 24
6 W	0447 1059 1726 2310	0.9 5.9 1.4 4.9	27 180 43 149	21 Th	0006 0606 1246 1854	5.3 0.8 6.1 1.0	162 24 186 30
7 Th	0535 1150 1819	1.0 5.8 1.5	30 177 46	22 F ◐	0105 0705 1345 1951	5.1 1.0 5.8 1.2	155 30 177 37
8 F ◯	0008 0631 1249 1919	4.9 1.1 5.8 1.5	149 34 177 46	23 Sa	0205 0808 1441 2047	5.1 1.2 5.7 1.1	155 37 174 34
9 Sa	0117 0736 1352 2024	5.0 1.1 5.8 1.3	152 34 177 40	24 Su	0303 0908 1533 2141	5.2 1.2 5.6 1.0	158 37 171 30
10 Su	0227 0844 1457 2127	5.2 0.9 6.0 1.0	158 27 183 30	25 M	0358 1003 1624 2228	5.3 1.2 5.5 0.9	162 37 168 27
11 M	0332 0950 1558 2224	5.6 0.6 6.1 0.6	171 18 186 18	26 Tu	0445 1054 1710 2312	5.6 1.0 5.5 0.7	171 30 168 21
12 Tu	0435 1051 1656 2318	6.0 0.3 6.3 0.1	183 9 192 3	27 W	0530 1141 1752 2354	5.8 0.9 5.5 0.6	177 27 168 18
13 W	0533 1147 1752	6.5 0.0 6.5	198 0 198	28 Th	0610 1223 1831	6.0 0.8 5.5	183 24 168
14 Th	0009 0627 1242 1845	-0.2 6.9 -0.2 6.5	-6 210 -6 198	29 F	0034 0650 1303 1909	0.5 6.1 0.7 5.5	15 186 21 168
15 F ●	0058 0721 1335 1937	-0.4 7.2 -0.3 6.5	-12 219 -9 198	30 Sa ◯	0112 0726 1343 1945	0.4 6.2 0.7 5.4	12 189 21 165
				31 Su	0150 0801 1423 2020	0.4 6.2 0.7 5.2	12 189 21 158

November

	Time	Height ft	Height cm		Time	Height ft	Height cm
1 M	0226 0838 1501 2053	0.5 6.2 0.8 5.1	15 189 24 155	16 Tu	0305 0939 1548 2153	-0.3 6.8 0.1 5.5	-9 207 3 168
2 Tu	0304 0915 1540 2129	0.5 6.1 0.9 5.0	15 186 27 152	17 W	0353 1029 1639 2247	0.0 6.5 0.3 5.3	0 198 9 162
3 W	0343 0953 1620 2207	0.6 6.1 1.0 5.0	18 186 30 152	18 Th	0444 1121 1729 2339	0.3 6.1 0.6 5.1	9 186 18 155
4 Th	0425 1036 1706 2255	0.7 6.0 1.1 4.9	21 183 34 149	19 F	0537 1212 1820	0.7 5.8 0.8	21 177 24
5 F	0514 1127 1757 2353	0.8 5.9 1.1 5.0	24 180 34 152	20 Sa ◐	0033 0633 1305 1912	5.0 1.0 5.5 0.9	152 30 168 27
6 Sa	0609 1222 1853	0.9 5.8 1.0	27 177 30	21 Su	0129 0729 1354 2003	4.9 1.2 5.2 0.9	149 37 158 27
7 Su ◯	0057 0713 1325 1954	5.1 0.9 5.8 0.8	155 27 177 24	22 M	0225 0829 1448 2057	5.0 1.2 5.1 0.9	152 37 155 27
8 M	0204 0821 1427 2054	5.4 0.8 5.8 0.6	165 24 177 18	23 Tu	0317 0926 1539 2145	5.1 1.2 5.0 0.7	155 37 152 21
9 Tu	0311 0928 1531 2153	5.7 0.6 5.8 0.3	174 18 177 9	24 W	0406 1017 1628 2233	5.3 1.1 5.0 0.6	162 34 152 18
10 W	0414 1030 1631 2251	6.2 0.3 5.9 -0.1	189 9 180 -3	25 Th	0454 1107 1713 2317	5.5 0.9 5.0 0.5	168 27 152 15
11 Th	0513 1130 1728 2344	6.6 0.1 6.0 -0.4	201 3 183 -12	26 F	0538 1154 1757	5.7 0.8 5.0	174 24 152
12 F	0610 1226 1824	6.9 -0.2 6.0	210 -6 183	27 Sa	0001 0621 1239 1839	0.3 5.9 0.6 5.0	9 180 18 152
13 Sa ●	0035 0703 1318 1918	-0.5 7.1 -0.3 6.0	-15 216 -9 183	28 Su	0043 0700 1319 1919	0.2 6.0 0.5 5.0	6 183 15 152
14 Su	0127 0756 1409 2010	-0.6 7.2 -0.3 5.9	-18 219 -9 180	29 M	0122 0739 1401 1956	0.1 6.1 0.5 4.9	3 186 15 149
15 M	0215 0848 1459 2102	-0.5 7.1 -0.1 5.7	-15 216 -3 174	30 Tu	0202 0818 1441 2033	0.1 6.1 0.5 4.9	3 186 15 149

December

	Time	Height ft	Height cm		Time	Height ft	Height cm
1 W	0241 0857 1522 2114	0.1 6.1 0.5 4.9	3 186 15 149	16 Th	0332 1005 1610 2219	-0.2 6.1 0.0 5.1	-6 186 0 155
2 Th	0324 0936 1602 2157	0.1 6.0 0.5 4.9	3 183 15 149	17 F	0418 1050 1655 2306	0.1 5.7 0.2 4.9	3 174 6 149
3 F	0409 1021 1647 2247	0.2 5.9 0.5 5.0	6 180 15 152	18 Sa	0505 1134 1742 2356	0.4 5.4 0.4 4.8	12 165 12 146
4 Sa	0458 1109 1735 2343	0.3 5.8 0.4 5.1	9 177 12 155	19 Su	0555 1219 1827	0.7 5.0 0.5	21 152 15
5 Su	0553 1201 1828	0.4 5.6 0.4	12 171 12	20 M ◐	0044 0646 1305 1915	4.7 0.9 4.8 0.6	143 27 146 18
6 M	0043 0656 1300 1926	5.2 0.5 5.5 0.3	158 15 168 9	21 Tu	0134 0742 1355 2006	4.7 1.1 4.6 0.6	143 34 140 18
7 Tu	0147 0800 1401 2025	5.4 0.5 5.4 0.1	165 15 165 3	22 W	0227 0840 1447 2058	4.8 1.1 4.4 0.6	146 34 134 18
8 W	0253 0908 1506 2126	5.7 0.4 5.3 -0.1	174 12 162 -3	23 Th	0320 0937 1539 2150	4.9 1.1 4.4 0.5	149 34 134 15
9 Th	0356 1012 1609 2227	6.0 0.3 5.3 -0.3	183 9 162 -9	24 F	0412 1032 1632 2240	5.1 0.9 4.4 0.3	155 27 134 9
10 F	0456 1113 1709 2323	6.3 0.0 5.3 -0.5	192 0 162 -15	25 Sa	0501 1123 1722 2328	5.3 0.7 4.5 0.2	162 21 137 6
11 Sa	0554 1210 1807	6.6 -0.2 5.4	201 -6 165	26 Su	0549 1211 1808	5.5 0.5 4.5	168 15 137
12 Su	0016 0650 1303 1902	-0.6 6.7 -0.3 5.4	-18 204 -9 165	27 M	0015 0635 1255 1853	0.0 5.7 0.3 4.7	0 174 9 143
13 M ●	0108 0741 1351 1954	-0.7 6.7 -0.3 5.4	-21 204 -9 165	28 Tu ◯	0058 0716 1339 1935	-0.2 5.9 0.2 4.8	-6 180 6 146
14 Tu	0157 0831 1442 2044	-0.6 6.6 -0.3 5.3	-18 201 -9 162	29 W	0141 0758 1421 2017	-0.3 6.0 0.0 4.9	-9 183 0 149
15 W	0245 0919 1526 2133	-0.5 6.4 -0.2 5.2	-15 195 -6 158	30 Th	0225 0839 1502 2059	-0.4 6.0 -0.1 5.0	-12 183 -3 152
				31 F	0309 0922 1544 2146	-0.4 6.0 -0.2 5.1	-12 183 -6 155

Time meridian 75° W. 0000 is midnight. 1200 is noon.
Heights are referred to mean lower low water which is the chart datum of soundings.

Appendix C

Baltimore, Maryland
Times and Heights of High and Low Waters

October

	Time	Height			Time	Height	
	h m	ft	cm		h m	ft	cm
1 F	0102	0.7	21	**16 Sa**	0108	0.4	12
	0646	1.5	46		0641	1.4	43
	1253	0.5	15		1248	0.1	3
	1930	1.7	52		1935	2.0	61
2 Sa	0141	0.7	21	**17 Su**	0202	0.4	12
	0715	1.4	43		0729	1.4	43
	1324	0.4	12		1333	0.1	3
	2005	1.7	52		2027	2.0	61
3 Su	0221	0.7	21	**18 M**	0258	0.5	15
	0746	1.4	43		0816	1.3	40
	1353	0.4	12		1420	0.1	3
	2044	1.8	55		2119	2.0	61
4 M	0303	0.8	24	**19 Tu**	0357	0.5	15
	0817	1.3	40		0907	1.2	37
	1427	0.4	12		1509	0.1	3
	2124	1.8	55		2214	1.9	58
5 Tu	0348	0.8	24	**20 W**	0454	0.6	18
	0851	1.3	40		1001	1.2	37
	1503	0.4	12		1604	0.2	6
	2206	1.7	52		2310	1.8	55
6 W	0436	0.8	24	**21 Th**	0553	0.6	18
	0933	1.2	37		1104	1.1	34
	1544	0.4	12		1704	0.3	9
	2255	1.7	52				
7 Th	0531	0.8	24	**22 F**	0008	1.7	52
	1025	1.2	37		0651	0.6	18
	1633	0.5	15		1210	1.1	34
	2345	1.7	52	◐	1809	0.4	12
8 F	0627	0.8	24	**23 Sa**	0107	1.6	49
	1128	1.2	37		0747	0.6	18
	1733	0.5	15		1322	1.2	37
◐					1922	0.5	15
9 Sa	0041	1.7	52	**24 Su**	0206	1.5	46
	0727	0.7	21		0837	0.5	15
	1242	1.2	37		1427	1.2	37
	1841	0.5	15		2033	0.5	15
10 Su	0137	1.7	52	**25 M**	0257	1.4	43
	0819	0.6	18		0919	0.5	15
	1356	1.3	40		1530	1.3	40
	1954	0.5	15		2136	0.5	15
11 M	0237	1.7	52	**26 Tu**	0342	1.3	40
	0907	0.5	15		1000	0.4	12
	1503	1.4	43		1621	1.4	43
	2105	0.5	15		2232	0.5	15
12 Tu	0330	1.6	49	**27 W**	0424	1.3	40
	0953	0.5	15		1035	0.4	12
	1606	1.6	49		1708	1.5	46
	2211	0.5	15		2323	0.5	15
13 W	0421	1.6	49	**28 Th**	0503	1.2	37
	1037	0.3	9		1109	0.3	9
	1701	1.7	52		1747	1.5	46
	2311	0.4	12				
14 Th	0506	1.6	49	**29 F**	0009	0.5	15
	1119	0.2	6		0538	1.2	37
	1754	1.9	58		1141	0.3	9
					1825	1.6	49
15 F	0011	0.4	12	**30 Sa**	0048	0.5	15
	0555	1.5	46		0610	1.2	37
	1204	0.1	3		1213	0.2	6
●	1845	2.0	61	○	1904	1.6	49
				31 Su	0128	0.5	15
					0643	1.1	34
					1245	0.2	6
					1939	1.6	49

November

	Time	Height			Time	Height	
	h m	ft	cm		h m	ft	cm
1 M	0209	0.5	15	**16 Tu**	0251	0.3	9
	0717	1.1	34		0757	1.0	30
	1319	0.2	6		1358	-0.1	-3
	2017	1.6	49		2100	1.7	52
2 Tu	0251	0.5	15	**17 W**	0339	0.3	9
	0753	1.0	30		0848	1.0	30
	1351	0.2	6		1450	-0.1	-3
	2055	1.6	49		2150	1.6	49
3 W	0332	0.5	15	**18 Th**	0428	0.3	9
	0835	1.0	30		0947	0.9	27
	1433	0.2	6		1543	0.0	0
	2138	1.6	49		2239	1.5	46
4 Th	0415	0.5	15	**19 F**	0517	0.3	9
	0920	1.0	30		1047	0.9	27
	1516	0.2	6		1642	0.1	3
	2222	1.6	49		2331	1.4	43
5 F	0503	0.5	15	**20 Sa**	0606	0.3	9
	1015	1.0	30		1151	1.0	30
	1611	0.3	9		1747	0.2	6
	2310	1.5	46	◐			
6 Sa	0554	0.4	12	**21 Su**	0021	1.2	37
	1121	1.0	30		0654	0.3	9
	1713	0.3	9		1257	1.0	30
					1853	0.3	9
7 Su	0003	1.5	46	**22 M**	0109	1.1	34
	0644	0.4	12		0740	0.2	6
	1232	1.1	34		1359	1.1	34
◐	1824	0.4	12		2003	0.4	12
8 M	0058	1.4	43	**23 Tu**	0201	1.0	30
	0735	0.3	9		0825	0.2	6
	1342	1.2	37		1501	1.1	34
	1939	0.4	12		2107	0.4	12
9 Tu	0154	1.3	40	**24 W**	0247	1.0	30
	0822	0.2	6		0907	0.1	3
	1448	1.3	40		1554	1.2	37
	2054	0.4	12		2207	0.4	12
10 W	0253	1.3	40	**25 Th**	0332	0.9	27
	0913	0.1	3		0946	0.1	3
	1549	1.5	46		1639	1.3	40
	2205	0.3	9		2300	0.4	12
11 Th	0345	1.2	37	**26 F**	0415	0.9	27
	0959	0.0	0		1024	0.0	0
	1645	1.6	49		1721	1.3	40
	2308	0.3	9		2349	0.3	9
12 F	0437	1.2	37	**27 Sa**	0456	0.8	24
	1045	-0.1	-3		1101	0.0	0
	1738	1.7	52		1800	1.4	43
13 Sa	0007	0.3	9	**28 Su**	0034	0.3	9
	0530	1.1	34		0535	0.8	24
	1133	-0.1	-3		1137	0.0	0
●	1830	1.8	55		1839	1.4	43
14 Su	0103	0.2	6	**29 M**	0114	0.3	9
	0618	1.1	34		0614	0.8	24
	1221	-0.2	-6		1212	-0.1	-3
	1920	1.8	55	○	1917	1.4	43
15 M	0157	0.2	6	**30 Tu**	0153	0.3	9
	0708	1.0	30		0654	0.8	24
	1309	-0.2	-6		1251	-0.1	-3
	2011	1.8	55		1956	1.4	43

December

	Time	Height			Time	Height	
	h m	ft	cm		h m	ft	cm
1 W	0232	0.2	6	**16 Th**	0313	0.0	0
	0736	0.8	24		0834	0.8	24
	1330	-0.1	-3		1432	-0.2	-6
	2032	1.4	43		2124	1.3	40
2 Th	0310	0.2	6	**17 F**	0356	0.0	0
	0819	0.8	24		0927	0.8	24
	1415	-0.1	-3		1524	-0.1	-3
	2110	1.4	43		2208	1.2	37
3 F	0351	0.2	6	**18 Sa**	0435	0.0	0
	0911	0.8	24		1020	0.8	24
	1503	0.0	0		1616	0.0	0
	2156	1.3	40		2249	1.1	34
4 Sa	0433	0.1	3	**19 Su**	0517	0.0	0
	1008	0.8	24		1119	0.8	24
	1559	0.0	0		1715	0.1	3
	2242	1.3	40		2331	0.9	27
5 Su	0517	0.1	3	**20 M**	0600	0.0	0
	1111	0.9	27		1218	0.8	24
	1701	0.1	3		1818	0.1	3
	2328	1.2	37	◐			
6 M	0605	0.0	0	**21 Tu**	0013	0.8	24
	1218	1.0	30		0644	-0.1	-3
	1814	0.2	6		1319	0.9	27
◐					1921	0.2	6
7 Tu	0023	1.1	34	**22 W**	0101	0.8	24
	0653	-0.1	-3		0730	-0.1	-3
	1327	1.1	34		1419	0.9	27
	1930	0.2	6		2029	0.2	6
8 W	0118	1.0	30	**23 Th**	0148	0.7	21
	0746	-0.1	-3		0814	-0.1	-3
	1432	1.2	37		1515	1.0	30
	2045	0.2	6		2133	0.2	6
9 Th	0217	0.9	27	**24 F**	0239	0.6	18
	0835	-0.2	-6		0901	-0.2	-6
	1535	1.3	40		1607	1.1	34
	2159	0.2	6		2231	0.2	6
10 F	0314	0.8	24	**25 Sa**	0329	0.6	18
	0928	-0.3	-9		0944	-0.2	-6
	1630	1.5	46		1652	1.1	34
	2303	0.3	9		2324	0.2	6
11 Sa	0412	0.8	24	**26 Su**	0415	0.6	18
	1021	-0.3	-9		1026	-0.2	-6
	1726	1.5	46		1735	1.2	37
	2349	0.3	9				
12 Su	0002	0.1	3	**27 M**	0010	0.1	3
	0507	0.8	24		0503	0.6	18
	1110	-0.4	-12		1108	-0.3	-9
	1818	1.6	49		1815	1.2	37
13 M	0054	0.1	3	**28 Tu**	0049	0.1	3
	0559	0.7	21		0548	0.6	18
	1202	-0.4	-12		1148	-0.3	-9
●	1907	1.6	49	○	1852	1.3	40
14 Tu	0146	0.0	0	**29 W**	0127	0.0	0
	0650	0.7	21		0633	0.6	18
	1252	-0.4	-12		1232	-0.3	-9
	1955	1.5	46		1929	1.3	40
15 W	0231	0.0	0	**30 Th**	0205	0.0	0
	0741	0.7	21		0719	0.6	18
	1341	-0.3	-9		1317	-0.3	-9
	2040	1.4	43		2011	1.3	40
				31 F	0241	-0.1	-3
					0808	0.7	21
					1404	-0.3	-9
					2050	1.2	37

Time meridian 75° W. 0000 is midnight. 1200 is noon.
Heights are referred to mean lower low water which is the chart datum of soundings.

64   *Oil Spill!*

Appendix D: Nautical Charts

San Francisco, California

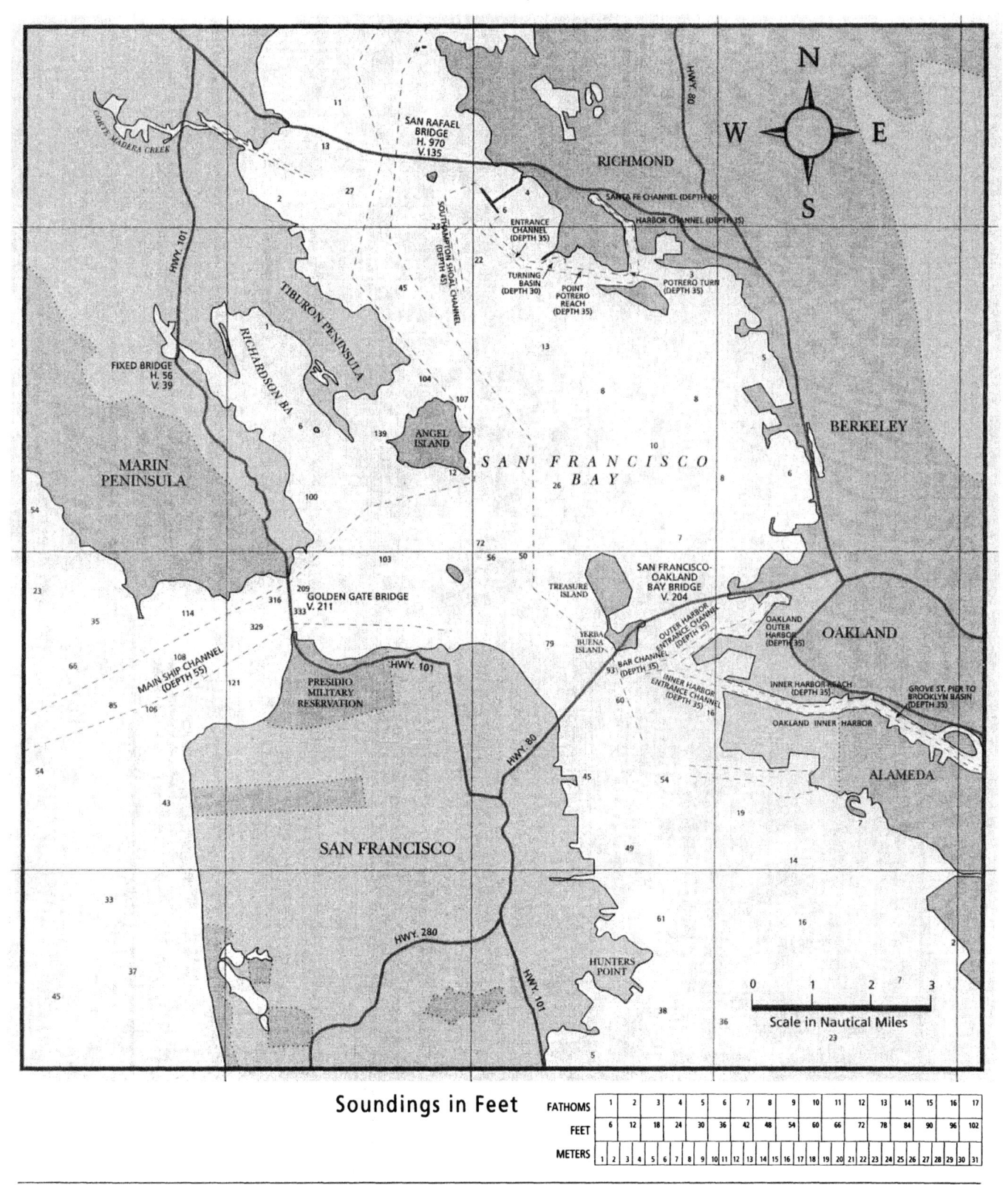

FATHOMS	1	2	3	4	5	6	7	8	9	10	11	12	13	14	15	16	17
FEET	6	12	18	24	30	36	42	48	54	60	66	72	78	84	90	96	102
METERS	1	2	3	4	5	6	7	8	9	10	11	12	13	14	15	16	17	18	19	20	21	22	23	24	25	26	27	28	29	30	31

Soundings in Feet

San Diego, California

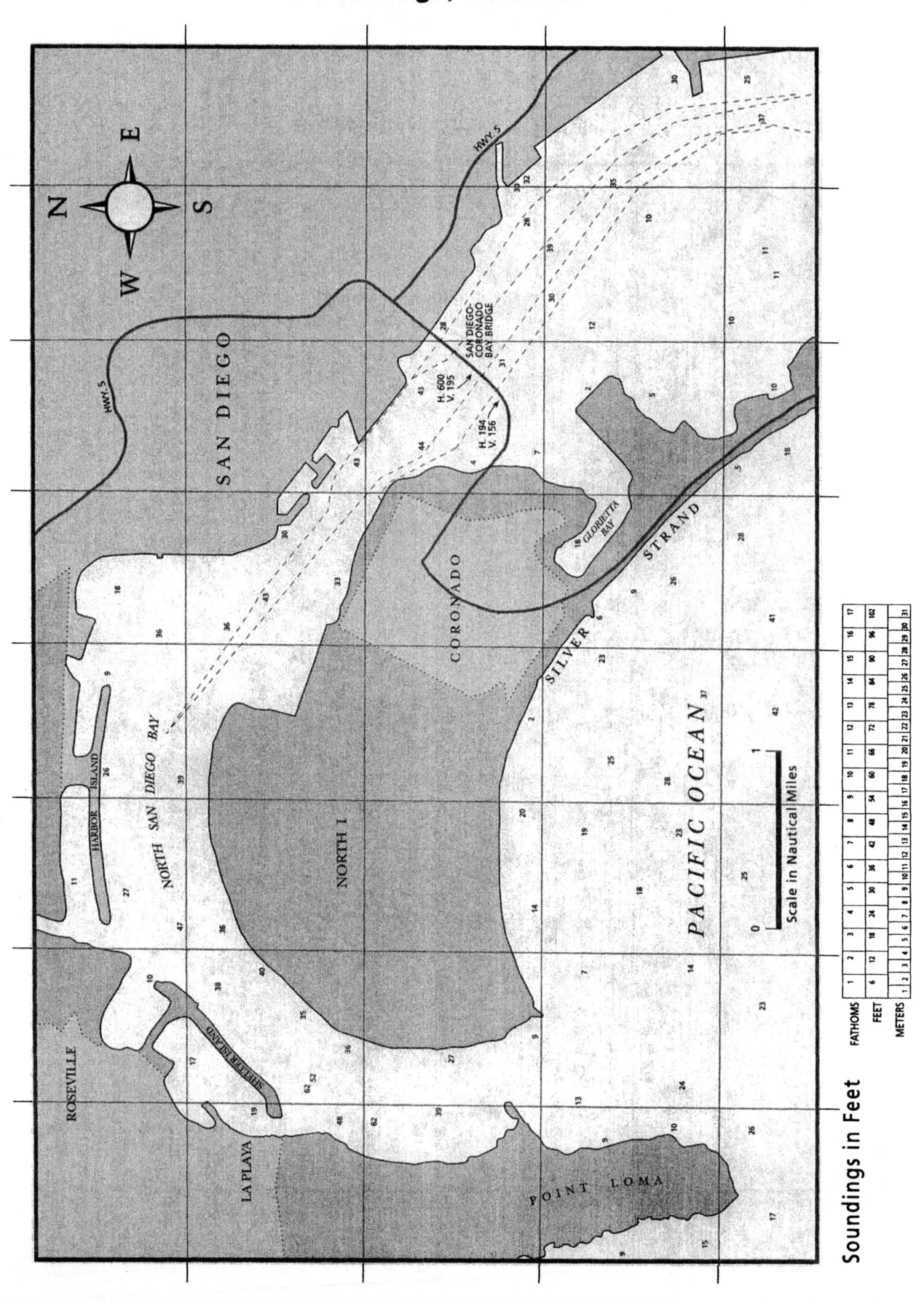

Soundings in Feet

66 *Oil Spill!*

Galveston, Texas

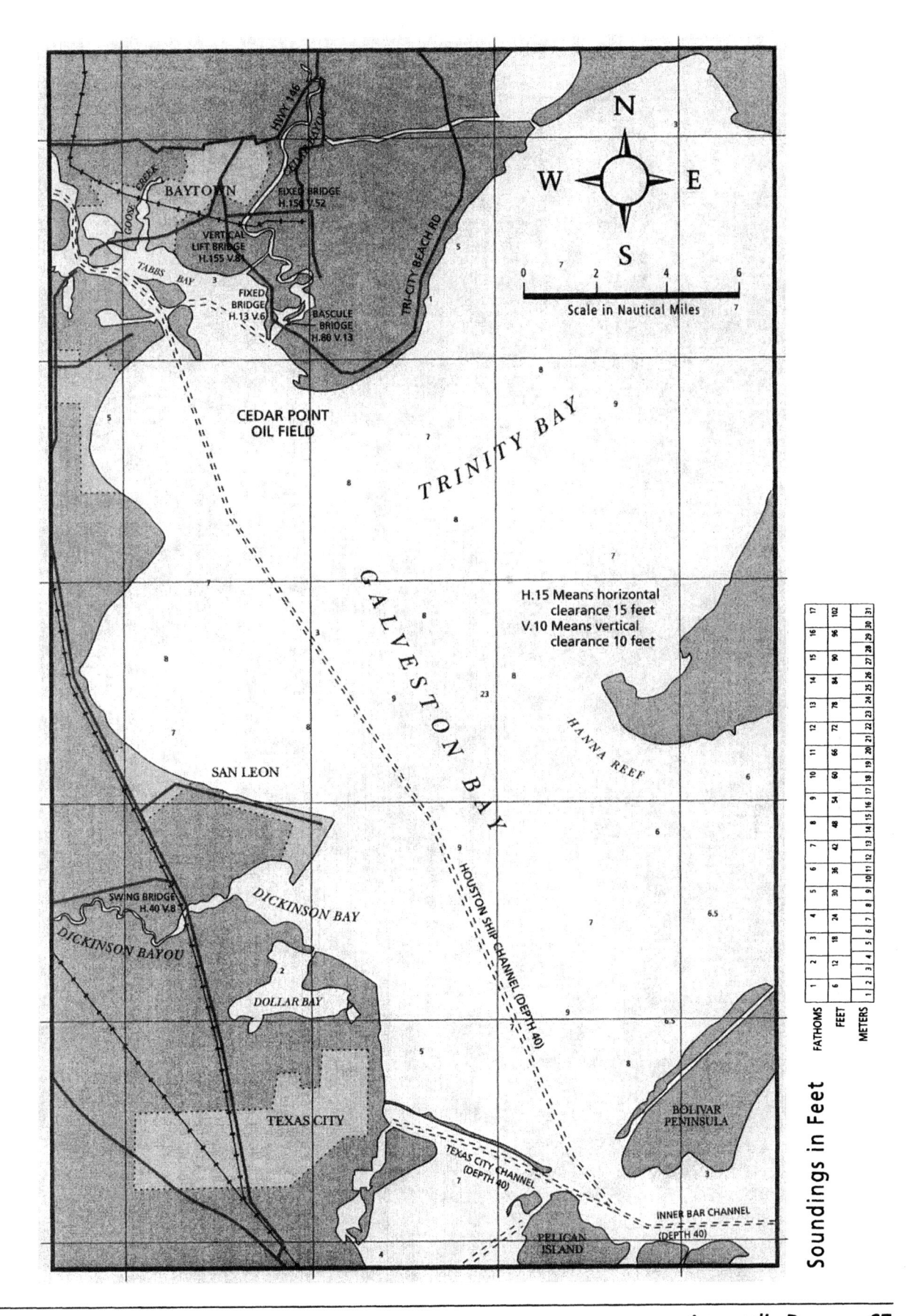

Appendix D

Pensacola, Florida

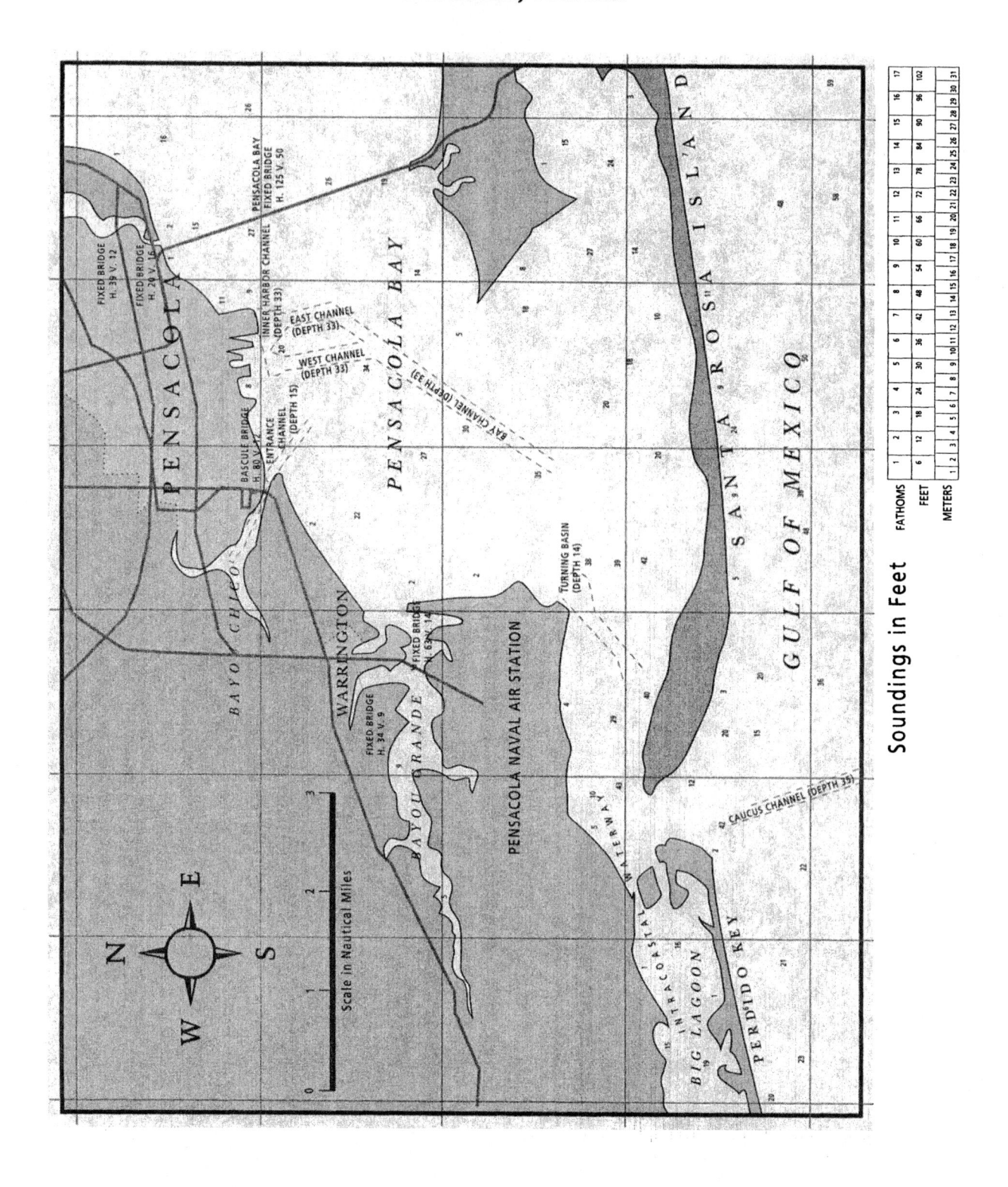

68 *Oil Spill!*

Charleston, South Carolina

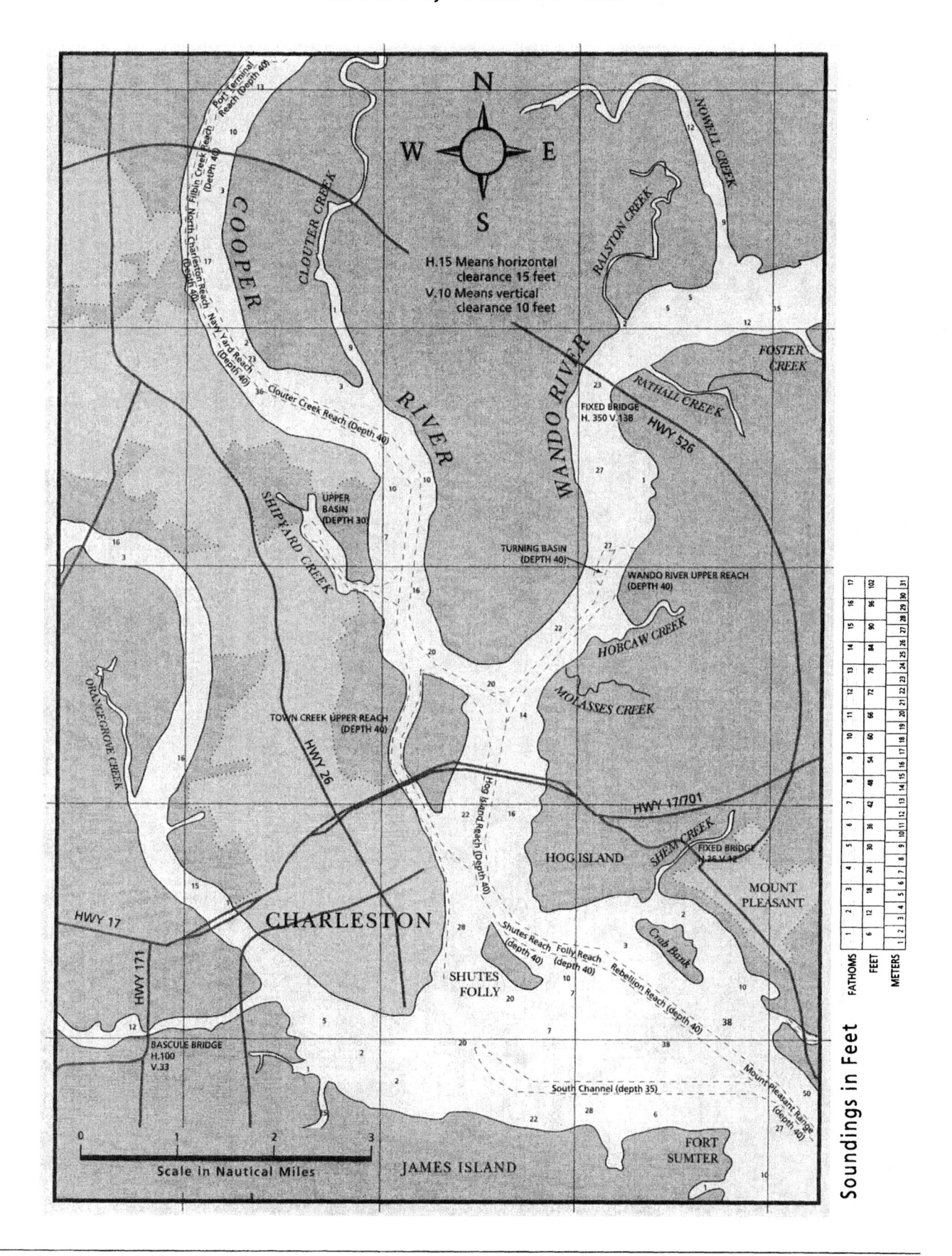

Appendix D

Baltimore, Maryland

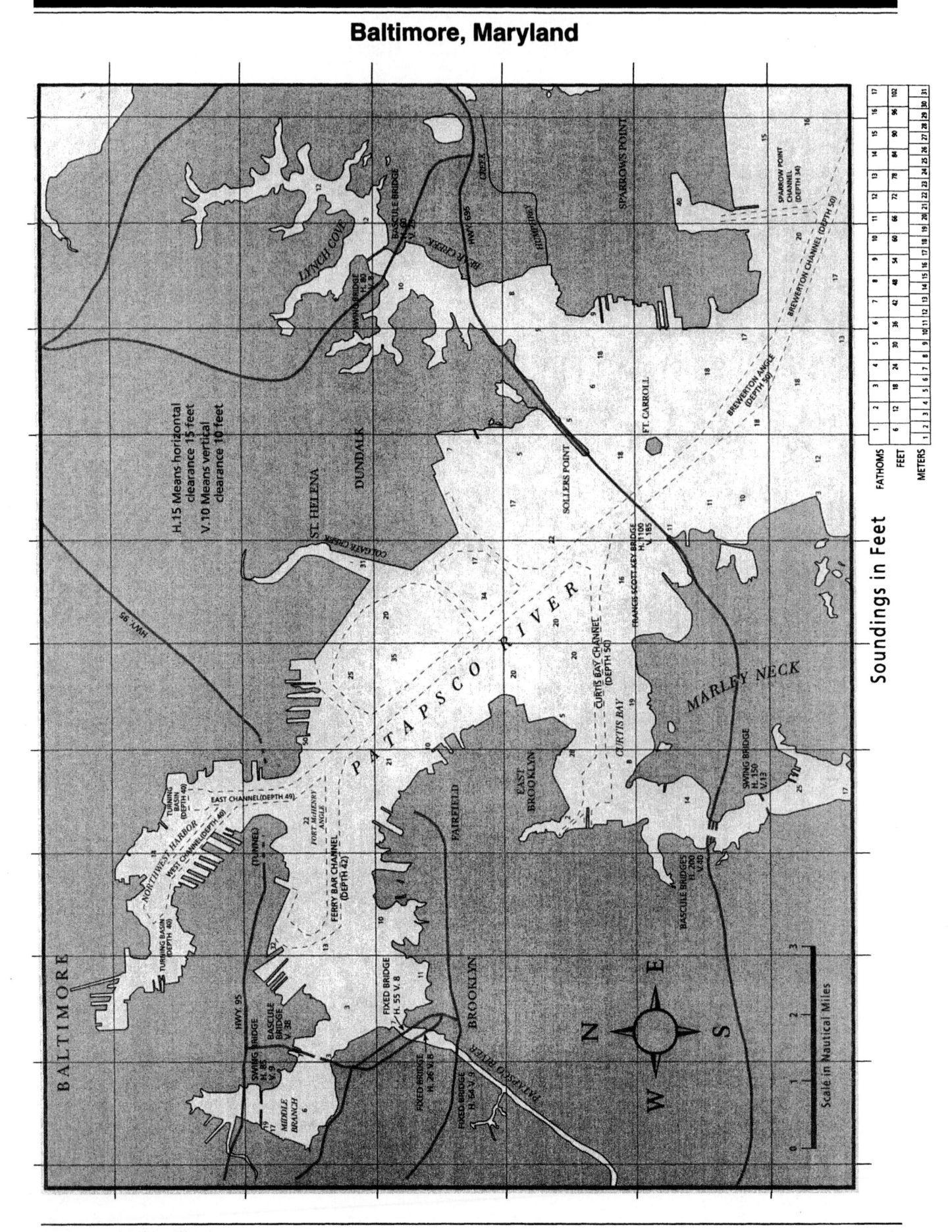

BIBLIOGRAPHY

Books for Students:

Farndon, John. *How the Earth Works.* New York: The Reader's Digest Association, Inc., 1992.

Kuhn, Karl F. *Basic Physics.* New York: John Wiley & Sons, Inc., 1979.

Lambert, David. *The Oceans,* Planet Earth Series. New York: The Bookwright Press, 1984.

Lambert, David. *The Oceans.* New York: Warwick Press, 1980.

Lockhart, Gary. *The Weather Companion: An Album of Meteorological History, Science Legend and Folklore.* New York: John Wiley and Sons, 1988.

Macaulay, David. *The Way Things Work.* Boston: Houghton Mifflin Company, 1988.

Nolan, Louise Mary, and Wallace Tucker. *Heath Physical Science.* Lexington, Mass.: D. C. Heath and Company, 1984.

Simon, Seymour. *Oceans.* New York: Morrow Junior Books, 1990.

Weiner, Jonathan. *Planet Earth.* New York: Bantam Books, 1986. (Companion volume to the PBS television series.)

Williams, Jack. USA Today's *The Weather Book: An Easy-to-Understand Guide to the USA's Weather.* New York: Vintage/Random House, 1992. Available through bookstores, or by calling (800) 972-0173. Also available: 8" × 10" overheads of *USA Today* graphics from book.

World Book Encyclopedia. Chicago: World Book, Inc., 1993.

Publications on Oil Spills:

Bioremediation for Marine Oil Spills. Office of Technology Assessment, United States Congress. Available for about $2 (order number 052-003-01240-5) from Superintendent of Documents, United Government Printing Office; Washington, DC 20402-9325; (202) 783-3238.

Related publications, slides, and videos (many showing on-the-scene footage) may be borrowed and copied from The Oil Spill Public Information Center; 645 G Street; Anchorage, AK 99501; (800) 478-7745 (within Alaska); (800) 283-7745 (outside Alaska); or (907) 278-8008; fax (907) 276-7178.

Also available from The Oil Spill Public Information Center: *Natural Resources Damage Assessment* and *Restoration Plan for the Exxon Valdez Oil Spill—1992 Draft Work Plan* (The Green Book) and *1993 Draft Work Plan* (The Blue Book). Prepared by Exxon *Valdez* Oil Spill Trustees.

SCIENCE SAFETY RULES

General
Follow all instructions. Never perform activities without the approval and supervision of your teacher. Do not engage in horseplay. Never eat or drink in the laboratory. Keep work areas clean and uncluttered.

Dress Code
Wear safety goggles whenever you work with chemicals, glassware, heat sources such as burners, or any substance that might get into your eyes. If you wear contact lenses, notify your teacher.

Wear a lab apron or coat whenever you work with corrosive chemicals or substances that can stain. Wear disposable plastic gloves when working with organisms and harmful chemicals. Tie back long hair. Remove or tie back any article of clothing or jewelry that can hang down and touch chemicals, flames, or equipment. Roll up long sleeves. Never wear open shoes or sandals.

First Aid
Report all accidents, injuries, or fires to your teacher, no matter how minor. Be aware of the location of the first-aid kit, emergency equipment such as the fire extinguisher and fire blanket, and the nearest telephone. Know whom to contact in an emergency.

Heating and Fire Safety
Keep all combustible materials away from flames. When heating a substance in a test tube, make sure that the mouth of the tube is not pointed at you or anyone else. Never heat a liquid in a closed container. Use an oven mitt to pick up a container that has been heated.

Using Chemicals Safely
Never put your face near the mouth of a container that holds chemicals. Never touch, taste, or smell a chemical unless your teacher tells you to.

Use only those chemicals needed in the activity. Keep all containers closed when chemicals are not being used. Pour all chemicals over the sink or a container, not over your work surface. Dispose of excess chemicals as instructed by your teacher.

Be extra careful when working with acids or bases. When mixing an acid and water, always pour the water into the container first and then add the acid to the water. Never pour water into an acid. Wash chemical spills and splashes immediately with plenty of water.

Using Glassware Safely
If glassware is broken or chipped, notify your teacher immediately. Never handle broken or chipped glass with your bare hands.

Never force glass tubing or thermometers into a rubber stopper or rubber tubing. Have your teacher insert the glass tubing or thermometer if required for an activity.

Using Sharp Instruments
Handle sharp instruments with extreme care. Never cut material toward you; cut away from you.

Animal and Plant Safety
Never perform experiments that cause pain, discomfort, or harm to animals. Only handle animals if absolutely necessary. If you know that you are allergic to certain plants, molds, or animals, tell your teacher before doing an activity in which these are used. Wash your hands thoroughly after any activity involving animals, plants, plant parts, or soil.

During field work, wear long pants, long sleeves, socks, and closed shoes. Avoid poisonous plants and fungi as well as plants with thorns.

End-of-Experiment Rules
Unplug all electrical equipment. Clean up your work area. Dispose of waste materials as instructed by your teacher. Wash your hands after every experiment.